POTPOURRI
The Art
of
Fragrance Crafting

Louise M. Gruenberg

DEDICATION

To my husband, David J. Walwark, for the intellectual, emotional, and financial support he has given to my creative endeavors.

This book is also dedicated to the member-customers and staff of Frontier Cooperative Herbs. Their support has also made this book possible.

Edited by
Jean Sherer and Frontier Cooperative Herbs

Cover Design: Judith Waterman
Cover Photo: Alan Miles
Illustrator: Liz Donahue

Published by
Frontier Cooperative Herbs
Box 299, Norway, Iowa 52318

Copyright © 1984 by
Frontier Cooperative Herbs.

All rights reserved. No part of this publication may be reproduced or transmitted in any form or by any means, electric or mechanical, including photocopy, recording or any information storage and retrieval system without written permission of the publisher.

Printed in the United States of America

Table of Contents

	Page
Introduction	5
History and Lore	7
FUNDAMENTALS OF FRAGRANCE	11
The Mysterious Power of Fragrance	12
Perfume Elements of a Potpourri	16
Fragrance Classifications	19
EQUIPMENT AND METHODS	25
Equipment	26
Blending Your Potpourri	28
Make It a Safe Experience	30
FORMULAS	31
FRAGRANT CRAFTS AND GIFTS	61
Showing Off Your Potpourri	62
Sachets and Pastilles	65
Fragrant Ornaments for Any Season	70
Create Perfumes and Colognes	73
The Complete Bathing Experience	75
Incense	79
Fragrant Wreaths	80

APPENDIXES 83

    I.   Quality and Effect Vocabulary 84

    II.   Standard Units of Measurement 85

    III.   Volume-to-Weight Chart 87

    IV.   FDA Restricted Usage List 91

    V.   Skin Allergy Test 92

    VI.   Fragrance Vocabulary 93

    VII.   Olfactory Perception Test 96

    VIII.   Standard Dilution Procedure 97

    IX.   Alcohol Dilution Chart 99

    X.   Sources of Essential Oils Used in Perfume 100

    XI.   The Secret Romantic Language of Flowers and Herbs 102

Introduction

Potpourri is a mixture of fragrant materials derived from seeds, flowers, leaves, roots, barks, woods, resins, gums, and natural or synthesized animal exudates.

A properly blended potpourri will last for months. Its uses are unlimited. Use your imagination—perfume the air with its continual fragrances, scent drawers and closets, make sweet-smelling stationery, add a final touch to room decorations with attractive baskets and bowls filled with your favorite mixture, or create personal gifts to share with friends.

Fragrance and beauty are not the only uses for a potpourri. Some blends of potpourri repel moths and other insects, while other potpourri mixtures protect furs and woolens in storage.

There are two ways to prepare potpourris: the dry method and the moist or wet method. The moist method uses scented, fresh materials which ferment and mature in a crock for several weeks. Wet potpourris retain their fragrance for a long period of time, but are not visually appealing. Dry potpourris consist of dried, scented, crisp materials concocted for fragrance as well as beauty. Herein the dry method of potpourri making will be explained in detail.

This book will give you formulas for mixing a variety of dry potpourri blends. The list of fragrance

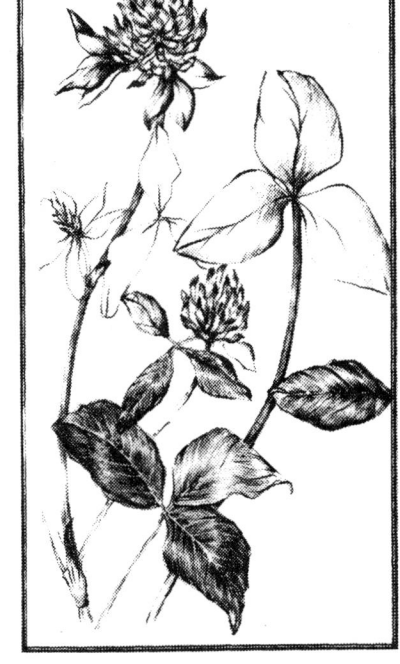

Red Clover
Trifolium pratense

categories, with their many variations, provides a guide that will allow you to select a unique, enjoyable scent. The book will also help the fragrance lover understand perfumery techniques.

A knowledge of perfumery, as well as practice in fragrance blending, will help you learn to adapt potpourri formulas so you can create other scented products such as cologne, bath salts, or incense. The base-blend system makes it easy for you to learn by experimenting, and eventually leads to the creation of your own distinctive formulas for any product.

Schools for perfumers are non-existent. The skill is acquired by experimenting with materials and techniques and analyzing the results. The true understanding of perfumery in potpourris comes from working with formulas, sniffing blends, and analyzing the often subtle scent changes when different materials are combined.

A sorting system, which divides the fragrances into ten categories, makes it easy to learn the craft. A formula for a base blend in each category is given, and five variations of each blend are explored.

You will be able to create blends from formulas from within one category or from all ten. The system is simple and fun!

History and Lore

Evidence of the use of fragrance materials goes back at least six thousand years. The tombs of ancient Egypt, excavations of long lost cities, trade records between kingdoms, and the accounts of contemporary writers provide us with a rich and interesting record of the uses of naturally-occurring fragrance materials, the only perfumes known to the ancients.

Originally, scented products were reserved for religious rituals. The priests were the first perfumers, and concocted incense, aromatic oils, and scented unguents for use in the temples. The Egyptian priests were renowned perfumers and created the first compound fragrance. Enormous quantities of incense were used in their rituals. At Heliopolis (City of the Sun), incense was offered to the sun god in special ceremonies three times a day. Gums were burned at sunrise, myrrh at noon, and a very expensive blend of sixteen herbs and resins known as Kyphi was offered at sunset. The effect was intoxicating and brought on religious ecstasy. Plutarch described Kyphi's effects, saying that it "lulled one to sleep, allayed anxieties, and brightened dreams."

The Hebrews learned the use of perfume products from the Egyptians. They also burned incense with their sacrifices, and used anointing oils as part of their rituals. Myrrh was used in purification ceremonies.

The value of scent to alter states of consciousness caused it to be incorporated into the rituals and ceremonies of Hindus, Buddhists, Shintoists, Muslims, and Christians. Incense, flowers, and candles were, and still are, the most commonly used forms of fragrance in worship services.

Although the priests of all religions tried to reserve the use of perfumes for the worship of the deities, and warned against the vanity of self-adornment, the merchants were willing to sell to anyone who could meet their prices. It was not long before royalty and nobility were indulging themselves. Eventually, anyone who could afford even the cheapest of scents did so, although

conspicuous consumption of these extraordinarily expensive items remained limited to the extremely wealthy. Since the ruling class almost always controlled the resources and directed political events, we have many incidental accounts of their use of perfumed products.

The Roman emperors were famous for their extravagance. They had saffron sprayed from fountains and used as a strewing herb. The emperor Nero (1st century, A. D.) was in a class by himself, though. Flowers rained down from the ceiling in his state dining room, and silver pipes hidden in the walls sprayed perfumes upon the guests. He had the palace floors covered with red roses. He burnt the entire annual output of Arabian incense gums at his wife, Poppaea's, funeral.

Cleopatra (in the 1st century, B. C.) also used fragrance in extravagant gestures. She was not particularly attractive, but she was skilled in the cosmetic arts and knowledgeable about the allure of perfume. The purple sails of the royal barge were drenched with an intoxicating, narcotic lily oil for her first meeting with Marc Antony. Shakespeare probably took his description of this scene from Plutarch, saying even "the winds were lovesick . . .." Cleopatra took care that Marc Antony was love sick, also; she had the floors of the palace spread eighteen inches deep with rose petals!

The use of fragrant materials eventually spread to Europe and England. Much of this "new knowledge" was brought home by the Crusaders between the 11th and the 14th centuries. Botanical materials were eagerly sought after and traded for in India, China, Japan, Arabia, Egypt, Israel, Persia, Assyria, Greece, and Rome. Regular trade routes were established; wars were fought to protect or conquer territories containing valuable plants.

The Italians became the best continental perfumers. When Catherine de Medici went to France to marry Henry II (in the 16th century), she brought along her perfumer, Rene', and an alchemist to compound her cosmetics.

Elizabeth I, queen of England from 1558 to 1603, enjoyed the fresh scent of strewn herbs and retained a woman at a fixed salary to provide her with materials in season. She also hired a husband-and-wife team to prepare floral distillations.

By this time, the techniques of distillation and enfleurage were well-known. Any industrious woman could plant a garden from which to dry materials for use in sachet and potpourri, and could distill toilet waters and essences from the fresh materials. The use of pure alcohol to create perfumes was unknown, but essential oils were expressed from plants, and the more delicate flowers were steeped in oil or wine to release their scents.

Such oils were used as part of the bathing ritual. Soap was unknown, and cleansing was accomplished by sitting in a hot bath to open the pores of the skin. Oils were massaged in and then scraped off, carrying the dirt and impurities with them while leaving behind a fragrant scent.

Guests were honored, and homes decorated with

fragrance in many ways. Scent performed the duty of soap, deodorant, detergent, and insecticides. Sachets were used to scent and to repel bugs from clothing and linens. Patchouli and vetiver were particular favorites of Indian women, while lavender and rosemary were popular on the European continent. Incense was used to fumigate rooms and to scent clothing. The Chinese and Japanese developed special racks to hang their robes upon for scenting. Herbal extracts were used for baths, hair, floor, and furniture-washing. Lemon balm and other plants were rubbed into furniture to polish it. Floors were strewn with plant material to discourage insects and rodents and to provide a soft place for folks without chairs to sit. Herbs chosen for this purpose were lavender, woodruff, hyssop, rue, tansy, basil, sage, thyme, marjoram, chamomile, southernwood, wormwood, rosemary, and sweet flag (calamus) leaves. Pomanders were made of many materials and sniffed to protect one from disease and infection. Since some plant extracts are germicidal, this may have had a positive effect. Favorite materials were cloves, cassia, musk, ambergris, benzoin, and orris.

The ancient peoples of the world have left us a very rich legacy of plant materials and effective ways to utilize them to create fragrance. Perhaps their innovative and eminently enjoyable uses of fragrance materials will inspire you, so that you too will want to improve your life with these sweet, invisible effects.

FUNDAMENTALS of FRAGRANCE

The Mysterious Power of Fragrance

A lot has been suspected, but very little has actually been proven about the effects of various fragrances on the human psyche and emotions. The search for an understanding of these effects has been going on for hundreds of years.

Marestheus, a Greek physician, wrote several books about the effects one incurred when wearing chaplets or garlands of various leaves and flowers. He noted that some combinations caused fatigue and depression, while other combinations seemed to refresh and encourage the wearer.

All classification systems, whether they are systems to understand the effects of scents on emotions or systems to classify the scents by their similarities, have been rejected by the scientific community. The inability to duplicate the anticipated results in a laboratory has led to this rejection. Both trained and untrained volunteers have been involved in experiments, but reactions to fragrances are so subjective that a system has not yet been proven to present a unified theory of olfaction, or scent.

Theophrastoes, in his writing, complained that odors were not effectively classified:

"We speak of an odor as pungent, powerful, faint, sweet or heavy, though some of these descriptions apply to evil-smelling things as well as to those which have a good odor."

Laboratory tests consistently prove that the sense of smell is subjective. Even though there is some agreement about whether an odor smells foul or fragrant, there is almost no way the individual odor can be placed into a specific fragrance category, since different people will describe it in different ways.

Some researchers speculate that this phenomenon is caused by odor "imprinting." Certain smells will remind us of people, places, things, or happenings. For some reason, odors seem to effect our memory and maybe even our learning process.

The science of the sense of smell is fascinating. With the discovery of pheromones (scent signals released by insects and mammals to communicate with others in their species), the science is undergoing a revival of interest. The question most asked by researchers is whether humans also release pheromones, and if we do release these scent signals, what messages are we sending and receiving?

The lack of a satisfactory odor classification system is complicating the work being done by researchers. However, Dr. John Amoore is making progress in attempting to define "primary odors" which would correspond to the primary tastes. Everything we eat and drink is flavored, either singly or in combinations of four primary tastes: sweet, sour, salt, and bitter. By identifying primary odors, a scientifically valid odor classification system could be established. It would then be possible for researchers to study the effects of fragrance by tracing the brain activity and noting the body's physiological response to each primary odor. Because the sense of smell is ten thousand times more sensitive than the sense of taste, it could be a long time before we have a complete understanding of odors and their effects.

Even though his method is not absolute, the emotional classification system developed by Dr. Paul Jellinek, a perfumer, may be the best guide to the effects of scent on emotion. Jellinek's categories cover basic and positive human reactions caused by certain types of scents.

Jellinek's first category includes materials with <u>Sex-stimulating effects</u>. These materials have blunt and intense odors, with waxy, fatty, alkaline, or rancid overtones. Unless diluted, their odors are usually unpleasant. When diluted, they bloom into low, sweet, deep, and warm fragrances suggestive of body scents. The effect can be arousing. Sex-stimulating materials were treasured by ancient people and have been used for thousands of years. Musk, having a strong, lasting odor, is the most familiar material in this category. Ambergris, civet, and castoreum — other fragrances of animal origin

— are materials in this category which are almost as important as musk. There are few plant materials containing musk-like compounds which can be used in potpourri. Ambrette seeds, costus root, and Canada snake root are probably the best plant materials to use for this effect.

Sweet, heady, soft fragrance materials, such as flowers and balsams, create a feeling of langour and relaxation. These materials, which can dull our senses and slow physical reactions, fall into the category of Narcotic-intoxicating. Too much of this type of material can cause headaches and nausea.

Mints, evergreens, citrus, and camphor scents can stimulate, awaken, and cause feelings of physical well-being. These fragrances, which belong in the Refreshing category, are sharp, clean, high, and piercing. Used in large amounts, these materials will clear sinuses and cause the nose to run.

Jellinek's final category is Stimulating, and most seeds, stalks, roots, woods, mosses, and even some leaves belong in this group. These materials have dry, spicy, and bitter odors. Their effect is said to provoke intellectual and physical stimulation.

Some materials will fall between categories. The Quality and Effect Vocabulary (Appendix I) will help you analyze these materials.

When you work with fragrant materials, you will find that some materials will

Rosemary
Rosmarinus officinalis

14

have qualities of more than one category. These will make wonderful blenders. Using materials from more than one category can smooth the differences in a potpourri. Combining materials from the Sex-stimulating and Narcotic-intoxicating categories, and from the Refreshing and Stimulating categories, will accent and intensify their effects. Since categories one and three or two and four are in disagreement, such a blend will be complicated in effect. It is important that you keep this effect in mind when you are creating a potpourri. Use materials based on the desired effect and intended purpose of the blend.

Although perfumers are limited in the range of effects considered acceptable, you do not have this limitation and your potpourri products can be created with special fragrances to fit every room in your home. Kitchen blends can be sweet and spicy, fruity, or citrusy. Try refreshing mints, evergreens, or even lemony blends for the bathroom. Make variations on a theme, creating blends that are alike for the living room and bedrooms. The decorative living room basket could contain a refreshing floral scent with a citrus note. In the bedroom try a similar floral with a hint of musk.

The formula section of this book gives many variations and ideas that you can use in experiments to create your own individual scent.

Perfume Elements of a Potpourri

When creating a potpourri blend, you need to first determine the main scent you want. This will be the "theme" or "melody" of your blend. The source of this scent may be only one material, or it may be several compatible materials. One thing to be aware of when combining materials is that each item has a different "scent strength." To achieve a pleasant, rounded blend you will want to combine smaller amounts of a very strong item with larger quantities of very lightly-scented items. In this manner, you gain a blend of materials with a single "scent strength" so they can be detected together at the same time — as one unified fragrance.

After selecting and mixing your theme scent, add the blenders. These will be fragrant materials which accent and strengthen your theme scent by creating a "top note" which will reach the nose first, and a "bottom note" which

will echo and underline the impressions given by your top and theme notes. The notes must blend harmoniously and be almost inseperable at the conscious level, yet if you have chosen your materials well, you will sense its subtle distinctions and the fragrance will "sing" to you!

In <u>The Science and Art of Perfumery</u>, Edward Sagarin describes a perfumer attempting to create a fragrance:

> When he creates, he seeks to blend all varieties of diversified odors into a single one. But when he smells, he seeks to choose all the component parts and smell them separately, and then all together.
>
> In one odor he finds a suggestion of another. He makes note that they may be interchangeable, and then develops their points of difference.

Perfume compositions need to be balanced for harmony, then "fixed" with materials that release the fragrance slowly and evenly. Fixatives, which are also fragrant, blend and draw together other materials in a potpourri to create a new fragrance from the distinct odors. They also will help the potpourri keep its scent for several months by "holding" the volatile oils. Without fixatives, the potpourri will be poorly developed and will fade quickly. They are an invaluable part of potpourri making.

The roots orris, calamus, angelica, and vetiver are the most commonly used fixatives in potpourri. Animal scents are also excellent. Others that work well in potpourri are: frankincense, myrrh, benzoin, labdanum, storax, balsam of Peru, sandalwood, balsam of Tolu, oak moss, reindeer moss, tonka beans, vanilla beans, and clary sage. Some materials, such as patchouli, sweet woodruff, costus root, and ambrette seeds are less valuable, but still useful as fixatives.

Each fixative should be chosen for its compatibility with a specific material used in the blend. A combination of fixatives can result in a higher-quality, longer-lasting potpourri. Some excellent combinations are: orris with florals, benzoin with florals and oriental blends, angelica with fruity and herbal blends, calamus in spicy scents, oak moss for florals and spice scents, and vetiver in herbal and woody blends. You are sure to find several personally satisfying fixatives.

According to Sagarin:

> A perfume is a symphony. To express a single emotion, no two composers, no two perfumers, would arrive at the same conclusion. The odor symphony must have harmony, unity, originality. It must evoke something in the heart of every man who has the sensory power of perception and the aesthetic power of evaluation. To each recipient of its message it will have a different meaning, but if it is a great creation, it will stir the soul to its very being, and will attain deserved immortality.

The final step in blending a potpourri worthy of Sagarin's description will be to add color and texture accents until you have the visual effect you want. You are sure to enjoy your first creation!

Fragrance Classifications

The ten fragrance categories which appear in this chapter have been selected because of their popularity. These categories are easily recognized by most people, and they are valuable to the perfumer. It is easy to classify and group materials according to their similarities. Comparing and contrasting materials in each category can also be done easily.

Classification by similarities and differences can be a helpful learning experience and can also focus your "mental" sense of smell. Once you have become familiar with the materials, it will not be difficult for you to remember them. Sense of smell is related to memory. Even after a long period of time, tests have shown an 80 percent retention in scent identification.

You can simplify your early attempts at potpourri blending if you create a fragrance that represents the overall scent of one of the following categories first, then experiment with the variations. Representative formulas for each of these categories, along with variations, are presented in later chapters.

TEN CATEGORIES

1. ANIMAL. The most powerful of the natural fragrances are those derived from animals. When making perfume, these intense fragrances are used in small amounts that often fall below the level of conscious perception. These fragrances have fixative properties (which will be discussed later), and act to soften, sweeten, dull, and harmonize with all the other materials in blends. They work well with most fragrances, but are especially good when used with florals, resins, spices, and woods.

The best-known animal fragrance is musk, which is taken from the scent gland of the male musk deer. Natural musk, with a strong, lasting odor, is expensive. Because musk is considered indispensable in perfumery, it has been successfully synthesized. The use of synthetic musk has also increased because the musk deer faces extinction.

Contemporary perfumers consider ambergris, civet, and castoreum to be of less value today, although each has been popular in the past. Natural ambergris is a waxy, lumpy, yellowish substance that sometimes washes up on beaches. However, it is usually recovered as a by-product of sperm whale slaughtering. Natural ambergris is thought to be an indigestible portion of the cuttlefish; it accumulates in the digestive tract of these sperm whales.

Civet and castoreum, bearing only a slight resemblance to musk, are extracted from the male and female civet cats and beavers. Even though civet cats can be kept in captivity, the collection process is painful for them. To gather castoreum, which is used in leather-scented perfumes, beavers must be slaughtered. Ambergris, civet, and castoreum are available in synthetic form, which are high in quality, and quite acceptable substitutes for the natural products.

2. CITRUS. Materials in this category have familiar fragrances: lemon, orange, grapefruit, and tangerine. Bits of peels can be used, or for a more concentrated effect, use the essential oils.

By using citrus-scented herbs, such as lemon balm, lemon verbena, lemon thyme, lemongrass, and orange mint, bulk can be added to a citrus potpourri. Citronella oil is extracted from a grass and has a pungent, aromatic citrus fragrance. You may know it as a mosquito repellent, or perhaps you have used it in candles as an outdoor insect repellent.

Bergamot oil has a peppery note of its own, but is best known for the distinctive, sharp, dry, and refreshing odor that is the trademark of citrus fragrances. It is used to scent and flavor Earl Grey tea.

Citrus materials have a cooling effect and are more volatile than any other natural aromatic. Because they evaporate faster, they make very effective "top notes" in potpourri blends. Citrus notes blend well with florals, herbals, mints, spices, and fruit blends.

Yarrow
Achillea millefolium

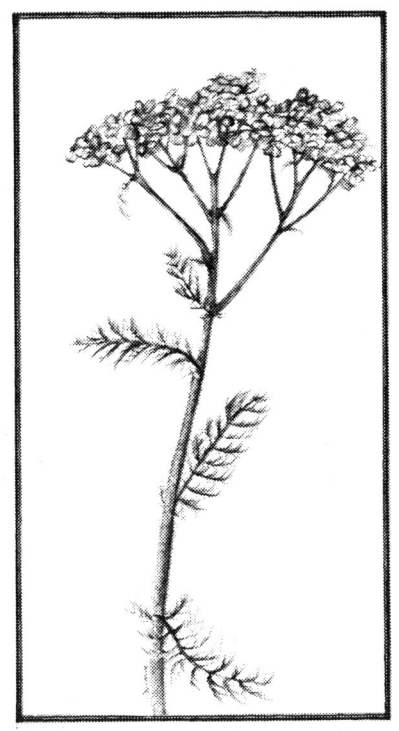

3. FLORAL. The popular flower fragrances belong in this category. Jasmine, rose, and orange blossoms are the three queens of perfumery, since they retain their scents when dried. They can also be used for color and texture.

Many flowers lose their perfume after they are dried. Some will even develop unpleasant odors. For this reason, carnation, gardenia, lilac, violet, lotus, magnolia, hyacinth, lily-of-the-valley, mignonette, and ylang ylang should be used in oil form. Real flower oils are extracted by enfleurage, a process of extracting perfumes by exposing absorbents to the exhalations of flowers. These oils can cost hundreds or even thousands of dollars per ounce. There are also high quality and reasonably priced synthetics available. Floral notes blend well with every other category. Let your taste in fragrance be the judge of how you will use them.

Certain dried flowers have little fragrance, but can add a marvelous visual impact to your creations with their wonderful colors and textures. Yarrow has big, creamy white pannicles; feverfew — another white flower — is shaped like a button. Globe amaranth, with its stiff straw-like texture and round shape, is red-violet. These flowers look very much like the common red clover which adorn roadside and field each summer. Calcatrippae flowers are tiny and resemble dried violets. You can get malva flowers in either a deep bluish-purple or black. They have a crepe-paper texture much like the dark, reddish-purple poppies. Hibiscus, which has a crisp texture, is a reddish-black flower. Kesu flowers are bright yellow-orange and look like dried daisies. Clover blossoms, which are white or red, really look more cream or violet-brown. For a delicate celadon green, use hop flowers which are attractively shaped. Spina cristi is a subtle apricot color and also has an appealing shape. Even though all of these blossoms have some fragrance, they are not strong enough to alter a blend or change its nature when used as an accent.

4. FRUITS. The sweet scents of ripe fruit—including strawberry, apricot, apple, banana, coconut, pineapple — are now available in synthetic oils.

Fruit fragrances, when used in small quantities, make effective top notes and are a pleasing addition to almost any blend. Try them with florals, woods, spices, and mints.

The leaves of fruiting plants, such as blackberry, blueberry, raspberry, and strawberry provide bulk and are also compatible with the fragrance in potpourris of this kind. A delicate fragrance, as well as color and texture, can be added by using rosehips, sumac berries, juniper berries, hawthorne, and elder berries. These materials also give a fruity look to your potpourri.

5. HAYS AND GRASSES. The scents from hays and grasses are light, dry, delicate, faint, fragile, and slightly sweet. Many dried herbs will have a grassy scent. Their fragrance is neutral and can be used in large quantities to create subtle effects and to add bulk. Sweet woodruff is the best material in this category. Deer's tongue leaves also have a sweet scent, almost like vanilla. Materials which will add a pleasant, light note to floral, herbal, and fruity mixtures are violet leaves, linden leaves and flowers, and uva ursi leaves.

6. HERBS. These materials are pungent, sharp and aromatic. They add a slightly bitter effect to a potpourri blend. Lavender is a popular standard in potpourris and sachets, because it adds fragrance, color, and texture. Sage, bay, and rosemary add beautiful texture and fragrance to herbal blends. Patchouli, having a unique earthy scent, has been a favorite in perfumery. Thyme, basil, rue, tansy, southernwood, and wormwood give distinctive fragrances to mixtures.

Herbs can be used dried or as oils. They blend well with florals, fruits, and resins. Many unusual herbs, such as tarragon and parsley seed oils, also have a place in perfumery.

7. MENTHOLS. Mints, evergreens, and camphors have distinctive, cool, breezy, and refreshing odors. Even though they are valuable in making perfumes, they must be used with discretion; otherwise they will overpower weaker odors. Try wintergreen for its sweetness. Experiment with the special softness of pennyroyal and the touch-of-hay scent of catnip. Eucalyptus has a scent almost like camphor. Peppermint and spearmint are other popular menthol materials. There are so many varieties of mint even botanists are often confused!

Dried mint materials are good for bulk and subtle effects. For more intensity, oils should be used. Menthol blends should be tried with citrus, spices, and florals.

Evergreen oils are available in pine, Siberian fir, thuja cedar leaf, and spruce scents. They can give any blend an exhilarating outdoor touch. Mix these oils with spices to create a special Christmas potpourri.

8. RESINS, MOSSES AND ROOTS. This category may be one you are not familiar with. Take the time to get to know these dry, low, sweet materials. They are also fixatives and are an invaluable aid to the perfumer.

Orris root smells faintly of violets, and oak moss is very sweet. For other scents in this category, try angelica, calamus, frankincense, myrrh, and vetiver. Resins, mosses, and roots blend well with all other materials and do a wonderful job of setting off the other materials.

9. SPICES. The materials in this category are well known for their use in perfume and, of course, in cooking. The singular sweet, rich, deep, and warm odors of spices add a special touch. Their interesting and varied shapes are equally helpful to the potpourri artisan. The more unusual cardamom, star anise, and tonka are all worth a try. Allspice, cinnamon, cloves, vanilla, nutmeg, mace, and coriander are great in blends with citrus. If you want an

unusual sweet and bitter scent, try oil of bitter almond. If sweetness is what you want, use anise. Spices can also be used in oil form.

Spices blend exceptionally well with woods, resins and roots, and animal fragrances.

10. WOODS AND BARKS. Trees are not only beautiful, many of them are also fragrant. Sandalwood is wonderful, and cedarwood has a well-known fragrant odor. Woods and barks can either be used in chips or as oils. They blend nicely with florals, animal scents, and resins.

These ten categories — plus a little imagination — will help you develop your own blends. Loosely speaking, children tend to favor the fruits and spices categories. Men often choose the resin-moss-roots and the woods-barks categories. Women tend to prefer florals, grasses, and citrus. Of course, the categories can overlap; each individual is unique, and personal preferences really are not restricted to particular categories.

Use your blends to create an environment: violets blooming at the edge of the woods, snow gently sifting over dried leaves, an early morning walk in a flower garden, the sweet smell of Grandma's kitchen at Christmas. Your potpourri can be a ticket to another time, a sweet reminder of another place, or a bright inspiration to energy and creativity.

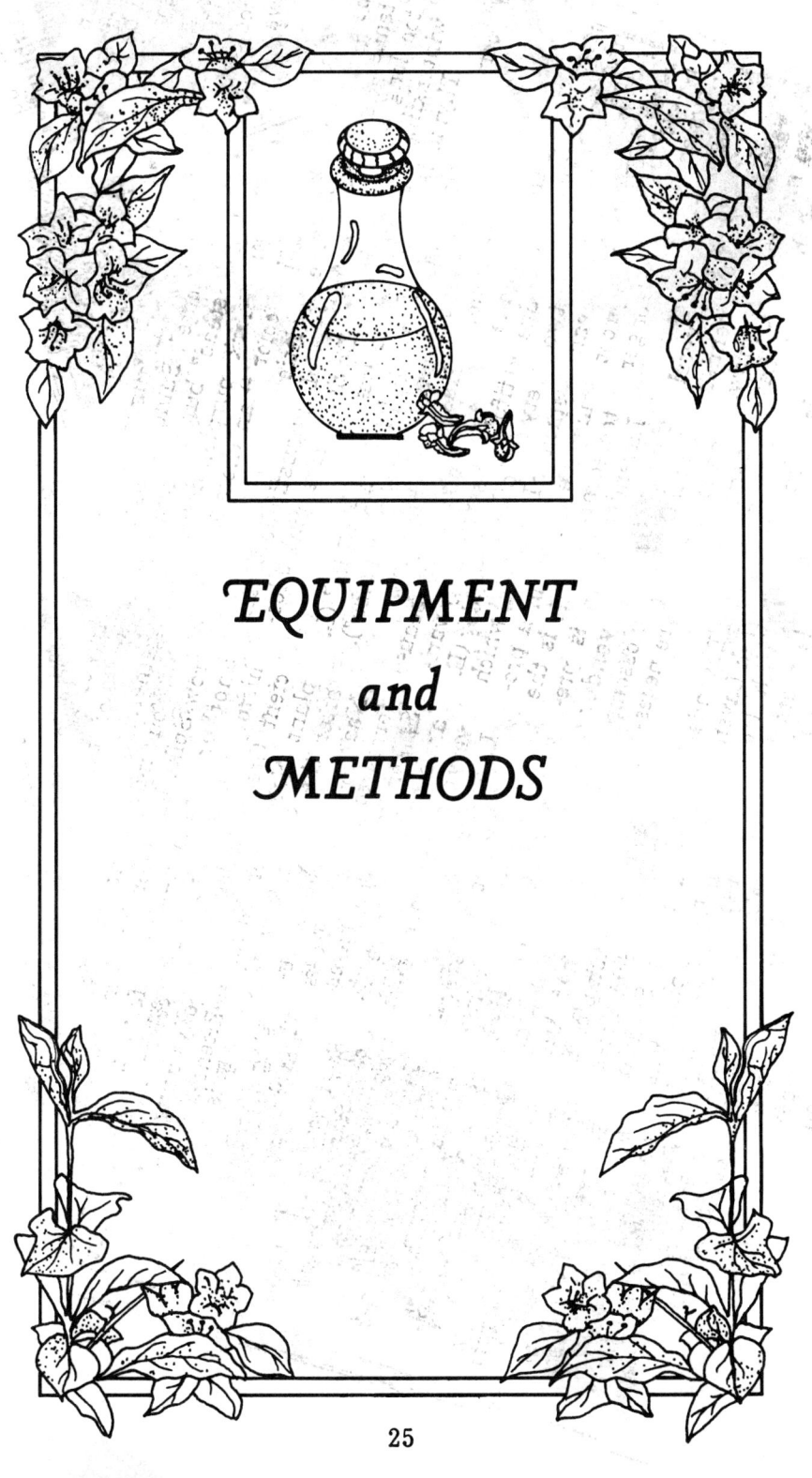

EQUIPMENT and METHODS

Equipment

You do not need a lot of expensive equipment to make a potpourri or sachet; most of what you will require is probably already in your kitchen.

For actual blending of your potpourris you will need: glass, stainless steel, or glazed ceramic bowls; stainless steel or glass measuring cups; and large stainless steel spoons or spatulas for mixing the materials. It is important not to use plastic items, as plastic can retain odors and can even be melted by some oils!

You will want to use glass jars with tight-fitting lids for storing materials and for aging completed blends. Jars protect the materials from insects and keep essential oils from evaporating. Amber or dark green glass jars work best, as they will keep out light which would otherwise fade the colors. However, any jar with a tight-fitting screw cap can be used. Label all jars and store them in a cool, dark, dry place.

Eyedroppers are very useful for dispensing oils. You should have one dropper for each oil you use, and it is a good idea to have some extras. Eyedroppers are inexpensive and are available at any drugstore. Other tools you are going to need when working with oils are small bottles (one-dram to four-ounce size). Two pint-jars of alcohol, either rubbing or grain alcohol, are necessary to clean the eyedroppers. You will use one to clean most of the

Passion Flower
Passiflora incarnata

oil from the eyedroppers and the other to remove any remaining traces of oil. Change the alcohol in both jars often. Do not let anything go to waste; if you use high-quality grain alcohol for cleaning, with a few additions you may be able to use it for cologne! Drain the eyedroppers and place them upside down in holes drilled into a small piece of wood to dry.

A mortar and pestle are helpful for "bruising" seeds to bring out their fragrance. A blender is good for making cosmetics, and a grain mill, spice grinder, or coffee mill that has been carefully cleaned out can be used to powder whole spices for pomanders and sachets. Use a small, sharp knife to slice vanilla and tonka beans, and shish-kebab skewers or chopsticks to pierce fruit for pomanders.

If you are going to sell your work, you will want to accurately reproduce formulas. Two scales should be used for this: a small one that weighs grams and ounces, up to a pound, and a larger scale that can weigh up to 10 pounds. The formulas in this book are developed by volume, so they are easy to reproduce. While volume measurements are not very accurate, you can easily convert the formulas to weight in ounces by using the Volume to Weight Chart in Appendix III.

Your own perceptions will teach you a great deal more than you can learn from books. You may find your most important piece of equipment is a notebook. Keep track of your experiments; note your reactions to individual materials or combinations. Notice changes each fragrant material makes when combined with other materials. These valuable notes can serve as inspiration and stimulate continued experimentation.

Blending Your Potpourri

Blending is mixing various materials together to create a fragrance. A perfumer is only satisfied when all the blended materials are working together to make one fragrance. When this happens, a special perfume has been created.

Your skill in blending will be developed by refining your sense of smell and your impressions of fragrant combinations of materials. These abilities can be gained only by experience.

This book has been designed to provide you with a series of formulas by category. Blending the base blends for each classification, and their variations, will give you the necessary experience to begin creating your own blends.

When blending fragrance products from a formula, first measure or weigh (see Volume to Weight Chart in Appendix III) the heavier materials into a mixing bowl. These heavier materials are roots, barks, and spices. The lighter, more delicate flowers and leaves are then added and the composition is stirred gently so that all ingredients are mixed. It is always better to use the whole form of flowers, leaves, and spices. Barks and roots can be used in the cut and sifted form. Powders have a tendency to sift to the bottom of your potpourri and are best suited for sachets and pomanders. Next, add your fixative. It is impossible to overuse fixatives. When making blends, use at least 15 to 25 percent fixative by weight. The last step is to sprinkle oils carefully over the entire surface of the mixture. Be careful not to "pour" the oils over the product. Add about half the specified amount, then evaluate the fragrance. Since oils are intense, you may need to adjust the specified amount of oil. Smell the mixture after each addition of oil and note the changes in fragrance and your reactions to them. These notes will be valuable when you begin to develop your own blends.

Oils can be added to the fixative in advance when using a formula with which you are familiar. Simply mix the oils and fixatives and place in a sealed glass jar. Aging this mixture for two to three days fixes the oils well and creates a longer lasting fragrance.

When you have added all the ingredients, gently stir the mixture and evaluate the fragrance. If you like it, what do you like about it? What is causing it to be unpleasant if you do not like the mixture? Is something missing? What? If you are curious about additions, use quarter-cup quantities and do a little experimenting, noting the changes in the fragrance, color, or texture of your blend.

Once you have the mixture you want, store it in glass jars in a cool, dry, and dark place for a two-week aging period. All perfume products need to age. This allows the different fragrances to blend and mellow. Evaluate the potpourri again after two weeks. If a particular material dominates the blend, make a note in your book and use less next time. If a scent has disappeared, then add more next time. Make these necessary adjustments and evaluate the fragrance again. When you know the materials and have developed the formulas and variations for several different fragrance classifications, you are ready to experience the truly fulfilling and creative aspect of this craft: creating your own blends which makes it possible to satisfy, to perfection, your own sense of smell.

If you are combining blends from "scratch", do not be concerned about adding materials in any particular order. Keep accurate notes of everything you do and, most importantly, of your reactions to the blend each time a new material is added. Watch out for odor fatigue. If you lose your sense of smell, go outside for a five- or ten-minute break. Be sure to use enough fixative -- 15 to 25 percent by weight — and add oils carefully, drop by drop. Too much oil can overbalance the precision of your blend, and you will need to increase the other materials to make up for your error.

There is no such thing as a ruined blend. By carefully adding other materials, you can alter the fragrance considerably and save the potpourri. When you are first experimenting, it is best to start out with small quantities of materials.

Make It a Safe Experience

Potpourri crafting is one of the safest hobbies you can pursue. Even children as young as five, with adult supervision, can make potpourris. The materials and equipment are not dangerous, especially if a few safety guidelines are followed.

Many of the materials used in this craft are edible, but it is best to store them away from small children. Be especially careful with items labeled "not for human consumption", or "not for human consumption except in alcoholic beverages". These guidelines have been established by the Food and Drug Administration for your safety (see Appendix IV).

Use spoons when stirring your mixtures, and if you are working with powdered materials, wear a pollen or dust mask. These safety precautions protect your skin and nasal passages from irritation. It is almost impossible to predict an allergy, and only exposure to materials will tell if you are allergic to them.

Because oils are so concentrated, they are more likely to cause irritation than other materials. If you are planning to use oils to scent bath salts or to make colognes, take the time to do an allergy test for the oils you intend to use. Allergy tests are explained in Appendix V.

Oils should never be taken internally. They are highly concentrated plant materials and should always be stored out of reach of children. If you find that a material causes skin irritation, stop using it in your cosmetic products and wear gloves when using the material in a potpourri blend. When displaying potpourri blends containing non-edible or FDA-restricted items, make sure children will not have access to them. Following these simple precautions will help make your potpourri-blending experiences safe and enjoyable.

FORMULAS

Feverfew
Chrysanthemum parthenium

This section contains the formulas for the base blends in the ten fragrance categories. Each formula will make about one gallon of finished product. Following the ten base blends are five variations for each base blend. Each variation requires two cups of the base blend. This leaves you six cups for use in other experiments.

The base blends are already complete potpourris. When you add color and texture materials, you are creating potpourris that are also visually appealing. If you want to experiment, leave the color and texture additives out of the base and add them only to the completed variations. By doing this, you control the color and texture of the finished product. When experimenting with this type of potpourri, use only about half, or a little less than half, of the oils.

ANIMAL (MUSK) BASE — QUANTITIES

Allspice	½ cup
Balm of Gilead buds	½ cup
Ginger root	½ cup
Orange blossoms	1½ cups
Rosebuds-pink	2½ cups
Woodruff	2½ cups

Fixatives

Calamus root	½ cup
Orris root	½ cup
Myrrh gum	½ cup
Sandalwood chips	½ cup
Tonka beans	½ cup

Oil

Musk	½ ounce

Color and Texture

Calcatrippae flowers	½ cup
Feverfew flowers	1½ cups
Linden leaves	1 cup
Malva flowers-blue	1 cup
Uva ursi	1½ cups

Total   16 cups

A sweet, soft, and mellow musk fragrance with a hint of flowers.

CITRUS BASE	QUANTITIES
Coriander seed	½ cup
Lemon balm	2 cups
Lemongrass	2 cups
Lemon peel	1 cup
Lemon thyme	½ cup
Lemon verbena	1 cup
Orange peel	½ cup

Fixative

Calamus root	1½ cups

Oils

Bergamot	1 tsp.
Lemon	1 Tbl.
Tangerine	1 tsp.

Color and Texture

Bay leaves	1 cup
Hibiscus flowers	1½ cups
Safflower petals	1½ cups
Spina cristi	1½ cups
Uva ursi	1½ cups
Total	16 cups

A sharp, high citrus note, dominated by the lemon oil. Invigorating and refreshing. Break the bay leaves into smaller pieces to even out the texture. Add kesu flowers for a pleasing touch of yellow.

FLORAL BASE   **QUANTITIES**

Allspice $\frac{1}{3}$ cup
Balm of Gilead buds $\frac{1}{3}$ cup
Lavender flowers   1 cup
Myrrh gum $\frac{1}{3}$ cup
Orange blossoms $\frac{2}{3}$ cup
Pennyroyal $\frac{1}{3}$ cup
Rosebuds-pink $1\frac{2}{3}$ cups
Rosebuds-red $3\frac{1}{3}$ cups
Violet leaves $1\frac{1}{3}$ cups
Woodruff $1\frac{2}{3}$ cups

Fixatives

Benzoin gum $\frac{1}{3}$ cup
Oak moss   1 cup
Orris root $\frac{1}{3}$ cup
Sandalwood chips $\frac{2}{3}$ cup
Tonka beans $\frac{1}{3}$ cup

Oils

Carnation $\frac{1}{2}$ tsp.
Jasmine   1 tsp.
Rose $1\frac{1}{2}$ tsps.

Color and Texture

Linden leaves $1\frac{1}{3}$ cups
Malva flowers-blue   1 cup
                                                                 ———
                              Total   16 cups

A simple and effective bouquet. The orris can be increased, and violet oil added.

FRUITY BASE   **QUANTITIES**

Chamomile flowers $\frac{2}{3}$ cup
Lemon balm $\frac{2}{3}$ cup
Lemon peel $\frac{2}{3}$ cup
Raspberry leaves   2 cups
Spina cristi $1\frac{1}{3}$ cups
Strawberry leaves $\frac{2}{3}$ cup
Violet leaves $1\frac{1}{3}$ cups

Fixatives

Angelica root $\frac{2}{3}$ cup
Orris root $\frac{2}{3}$ cup

Oils

Coriander   5 drops
Lime   10 drops
Strawberry   20 drops
Tangerine   10 drops

Color and Texture

Elder berries   1 cup
Hawthorne berries $\frac{2}{3}$ cup
Juniper berries   1 cup
Linden leaves $1\frac{1}{3}$ cups
Rosehips   1 cup
Sumac berries $\frac{2}{3}$ cup
Uva ursi $1\frac{2}{3}$ cups
                                                     ———
                                       Total   16 cups

A soft, sweet, fruity fragrance. A nice note for florals and herbals.

HAY-SCENTED BASE QUANTITIES

Alfalfa leaves	⅓ cup
Chamomile flowers	1⅓ cups
Clover blossoms–red	1⅓ cups
Hops flowers	⅔ cup
Orange blossoms	1 cup
Rosebuds–pink	1 cup
Rosebuds–red	1⅓ cups
Rue	⅓ cup
Southernwood	⅓ cup
Violet leaves	⅔ cup
Woodruff	2⅔ cups
Wormwood	⅓ cup

Fixatives

Orris root	1 cup
Tonka beans	⅓ cup
Vanilla bean	1 bean cut in ¼" sections

Oil

Violet	1 tsp.

Color and Texture

Calcatrippae flowers	⅔ cup
Globe Amaranth flowers	⅔ cup
Malva flowers–blue	1 cup
Yarrow flowers	1 cup

Total 16 cups

A pleasingly sweet, neutral fragrance of a grassy/cut hay nature. Very good with any floral oils.

HERB BASE	QUANTITIES
Bay leaves	2 cups
Coriander seed	$\frac{1}{2}$ cup
Hyssop	$\frac{1}{4}$ cup
Lavender flowers	2 cup
Lemon thyme	1 cup
Licorice mint (Anise hyssop)	$\frac{1}{4}$ cup
Patchouli	$\frac{3}{4}$ cup
Rosemary	1 cup
Sage	$2\frac{1}{2}$ cups
Tansy	$\frac{1}{4}$ cup
Thyme	$\frac{1}{4}$ cup

Fixatives

Angelica root	1 cup
Calamus root	$\frac{1}{4}$ cup

Oils

Bay	$\frac{1}{4}$ tsp.
Lavender	1 tsp.
Marjoram	$\frac{1}{4}$ tsp.
Rosemary	$\frac{1}{2}$ tsp.

Color and Texture

Calcatrippae flowers	$1\frac{1}{2}$ cups
Malva flowers-blue	$1\frac{1}{2}$ cups
Yarrow flowers	1 cup
Total	16 cups

A very pungent herbal, almost mentholated fragrance with a clean, refreshing scent. If this is too strong for you, reduce the oils by one half. Feverfew blossoms may be added as a white accent.

MENTHOL BASE   **QUANTITIES**

Catnip	1/3 cup
Eucalyptus	1/3 cup
Lemon balm	2/3 cup
Licorice mint (Anise hyssop)	2/3 cup
Patchouli	1/3 cup
Pennyroyal	2 cups
Peppermint	1/3 cup
Spearmint	1/3 cup
Wintergreen	1/3 cup
Woodruff	1 1/3 cups

Fixatives

Calamus root	2/3 cup
Vetiver root	2 cups

Oils

Pennyroyal	1/2 tsp.
Vetiver	1/2 tsp.

Color and Texture

Globe Amaranth flowers	2/3 cup
Malva flowers-blue	1 2/3 cups
Poppy flowers-red	1 cup
Senna leaves	1 cup
Uva ursi	1 1/3 cups
Yarrow flowers	1 cup

                                       Total   16 cups

A mellow, earthy mint scent. Crisp and revitalizing.

RESIN BASE   **QUANTITIES**

Balm of Gilead buds   1 cup
Rosebuds-red   3 cups
Woodruff   1½ cups

Fixatives

Benzoin gum   ½ cup
Frankincense   ½ cup
Myrrh gum   ½ cup
Oak moss   2 cups
Orris root   ½ cup
Tonka beans   ½ cup

Color and Texture

Linden leaves   2 cups
Malva flowers-blue   1 cup
Senna leaves   ½ cup
Uva ursi   1½ cups
Yarrow flowers   1 cup
                                                    ─────────
                          Total   16 cups

A dry, musty, almost neutral scent. A good base for other fragrances or additional oils.

SPICE BASE	QUANTITIES
Allspice	1½ cups
Anise	½ cup
Balm of Gilead buds	1 cup
Cinnamon	2 cups
Cloves	½ cup
Ginger root	1 cup

Fixatives

Calamus root	½ cup
Oak moss	3 cups
Orris root	½ cup
Sandalwood chips	1 cup
Tonka beans	½ cup
Vanilla bean	½ bean cut into ¼" sections

Oils

Allspice	1½ tsps.
Cinnamon	¾ tsp.
Clove	¾ tsp.
Tangerine	¾ tsp.

Color and Texture

Broom flowers	1 cup
Calendula	½ cup
Elder flowers	½ cup
Feverfew flowers	1½ cups
Yarrow flowers	½ cup
Total	16 cups

A sweet, soft, almost honey-scented spice. For a sharper spice fragrance, omit the broom and elder flowers, as they add the honey scent.

WOODY BASE   QUANTITIES

Bayberry bark	½ cup
Cedarwood chips	1½ cups
Cherry bark	½ cup
Cubeb berries	1 cup
Licorice root	½ cup
Linden leaves	2 cups
Patchouli	2 cups
Sarsaparilla root	½ cup
Sassafras root	1 cup

Fixatives

Angelica root	½ cup
Calamus root	½ cup
Sandalwood chips	1½ cups
Vetiver root	1 cup

Oils

Birch	¼ tsp.
Cedarwood	1¼ tsps.
Lavender	¾ tsp.
Sandalwood	4½ tsps.
Sassafras	½ tsp.

Color and Texture

Broom flowers	1 cup
Feverfew flowers	½ cup
Pine cones	½ cup
Tilia star flowers	½ cup
Uva ursi	½ cup

                            Total   16 cups

A sharp, earthy, and pungent scent. This would go well with any evergreen oil.

ANIMAL (MUSK) BASE VARIATIONS

Mellow Musk (musk & citrus)

2 cups musk base
2 cups hibiscus flowers
1 cup orange peel
1 cup lemon peel

½ cup sumac berries
½ cup angelica root
1 tsp. tangerine oil

The musk softens the piercing, sharp quality of the citrus to create a very soothing, mild fragrance with a soft citrus note. Increase the oil or try adding bergamot and/or lime oil. Sandalwood would make a good addition, as would allspice. Floral oils, especially rose oil, would be compatible. Try lavender flowers and oil.

Mellifluous Musk (musk & floral)

2 cups musk base
2 cups sandalwood
2 cups pink rosebuds
1 cup orange blossoms

½ cup orris root
½ cup benzoin gum
½ tsp. carnation oil

A soft floral with a spicy carnation note and the mellowing influence of sandalwood. Experiment with this formula by adding other floral oils. Allspice and cinnamon chips or oil could be added. Vanilla would sweeten and warm, and ginger would add a dry and spicy note. The visual effect would be enhanced with the addition of linden leaves, spina cristi, uva ursi leaves, and more roses or other blossoms.

Marvelous Musk (musk & fruity)

2 cups musk base
2 cups violet leaves
1½ cups linden leaves
½ cup coriander seed
½ cup allspice
½ cup anise seed

½ cup orange peel
½ cup angelica root
½ tsp. heliotrope oil
¼ tsp. strawberry oil
¼ tsp. bitter almond oil

You may not like the almond oil, as it has a very bitter quality. Its character changes after aging, losing the intrusive quality. The eventual effect is a soft, sweet, just barely fruity fragrance. Increase the fruity effect with the addition of more fruit oils. Try apricot for a sweeter note and add vanilla and tonka, too. Add rosehips, juniper berries, spina cristi, linden leaves, uva ursi, and flower blossoms for a prettier look.

Milk Musk (musk & hay scent)

2 cups musk base
2 cups woodruff
1 cup hyssop
1 cup rue
1 cup catnip

½ cup wormwood
½ cup oak moss
½ vanilla bean
chopped into ¼" pieces
and bruised in a mortar

This is a very mild fragrance with a definite cut-grass note. Increase the sweetness with vanilla, tonka, more oak moss and woodruff. You can add rosebuds, orange blossoms, sandalwood, violet or other floral oils. Calcatrippae, blue malva flowers, heather flowers, linden leaves, and uva ursi can be added to improve the visual effect.

Magic Musk (musk & herb)

2 cups musk base
2 cups lavender flowers

2 cups rosemary
2 cups vetiver root

A very soft, sweet, herbal fragrance. Oak moss would increase the sweetness. Add lavender oil to intensify the herbal note, or try sage, juniper, and/or patchouli oils. Feverfew, kesu, spina cristi, calcatrippae, and blue malva flowers would add some needed color.

CITRUS BASE VARIATIONS

Caress Citrus (citrus & floral)

2 cups citrus base
3 cups red rosebuds
2 cups woodruff
½ cup oak moss
¼ cup orris root
¼ cup sliced tonka beans

5 drops magnolia oil
10 drops each:
   jasmine,
   honeysuckle,
   grapefruit oil
20 drops tangerine oil

This is a sweet, but not overpowering floral with a nice touch of citrus. To decrease the sweetness, increase the grapefruit oil, add bergamot oil, ginger root, and cubeb berries. Bay leaves could be added to that variation for fragrance and texture. Increase the sweetness with oak moss, vanilla, and tonka; and add allspice, cinnamon, and cloves for a spicy note. Add your choice of flower blossoms for color.

Captivating Citrus (citrus & fruit)

2 cups citrus base
2 cups lemon peel
1½ cups uva ursi
1¼ cups chamomile
1 cup raspberry leaf

¼ cup angelica root
15 drops strawberry oil
10 drops sweet orange oil
5 drops lime oil

A sweet and tangy mixture. Increase the tartness with sumac berries, rosehips, and hibiscus flowers. Experiment with other fruit and citrus oils, and try bitter almond oil in this blend. Sweeten with allspice berries and cinnamon. Add bay leaves for fragrance and texture, linden leaves and kesu flowers for color and shape.

Chimerical Citrus (citrus & hay)

2 cups citrus base
2½ cups woodruff
2 cups red clover blossoms
1 cup violet leaves

½ cup orris root
½ tsp. violet oil
¼ tsp. lemongrass oil

This fragrance is elusive. The first impression is sweet, but the second is tart. Increase the sweetness with broom flowers, roses, orange blossoms, vanilla, and tonka. Sandalwood and benzoin would also be nice. Any floral oil could be added. Yarrow, heather, globe amaranth flowers, linden, and uva ursi leaves would enhance the appearance of the blend.

Charming Citrus (citrus and herbal)

2 cups citrus base
3 cups lavender flowers
1½ cups orange peel
1 cup sage

½ cup calamus root
½ tsp. bergamot oil
¼ tsp. lavender oil

A pleasant lavender with the barest hint of citrus. Add bergamot oil and try various herbal oils. For fragrance and texture, add bay leaves, rosemary, and lemon thyme. Add feverfew, yarrow, spina cristi, linden leaves, and blue malva for color.

Chilled Citrus (citrus & menthol)

2 cups citrus base
2 cups pennyroyal
2 cups wintergreen
1 cup orange peel

½ cup peppermint
½ cup calamus root
1 tsp. orange oil
6 drops pennyroyal oil

A cool and breezy combination. Increase the mentholated feeling with additional pennyroyal, peppermint oil, or cajeput oil. Lemongrass and tangerine oil would add to the overall softness. Cloves would add a sharp and spicy touch. Make it more visually attractive by adding flower blossoms and leaves.

FLORAL BASE VARIATIONS

Fabulous Floral (floral & fruit)

2 cups floral base
2 cups spina cristi
1 cup chamomile
1 cup heather flowers
½ cup elder berries

½ cup sumac berries
½ cup juniper berries
½ cup vetiver root
8 drops heliotrope oil
6 drops strawberry oil

A subtle and pleasing scent. Other fruit and flower oils could be added to increase the intensity of the fragrance. Lemon and orange peel, spices, vanilla beans, rosebuds, and sandalwood are all worth trying. Blue and black malva, uva ursi, and poppy flowers would give more color and texture.

Fairy Floral (floral & hay)

2 cups floral base
2 cups woodruff
2 cups oak moss

1 cup elder flowers
1 cup Canada snake root

All hay scents are subtle and elusive. This one has a sweet note derived from the oak moss and woodruff. Any floral oils would be compatible with this blend. Resins, sandalwood, musk oil, and tonka beans, as well as spices, would be pleasing additions. It needs flower blossoms and leaves to heighten the visual effect.

Flair Floral (floral & herb)

2 cups floral base
2 cups lavender flowers
1 cup sage
1 cup thyme
1 cup rosemary

1 cup vetiver root
6 drops oregano oil
20 drops patchouli oil
20 drops lavender oil
10 drops honeysuckle oil

This blend has a simultaneously sweet and bitter effect caused by the contrast of flower oils with oregano oil. If you leave out the oregano, you may have to decrease the quantities of the other oils. Bay leaves, patchouli leaf, and yerba santa would add to the herbal effect; rosebuds, orange blossoms, and jasmine flowers would add fragrance and color.

Flashy Floral (floral & menthol)

2 cups floral base
2 cups wintergreen
2 cups pennyroyal
1 cup birch bark

½ cup cloves
½ cup calamus root
12 drops gardenia oil
6 drops pennyroyal oil

Wintergreen and birch bark give this blend a sweet, rather than a mentholated, effect. To increase the sweetness still further, add tonka, vanilla, oak moss, and more floral oils. To increase the mentholated effect, substitute peppermint for the wintergreen. Citrus oils and peels, also spice oils and pieces, would be worth experimenting with. Rosebuds, malva flowers, calcatrippae, and leaves would enhance the texture and color.

Fantasia Floral (floral & resin)

2 cups floral base
2 cups rosebuds
2 cups balm of Gilead buds

1 cup benzoin gum
½ cup frankincense
½ cup myrrh gum

This soft, balsamic scent could be powdered and burned as an incense. Other floral oils could be added, as well as tonka, vanilla, oak moss, and sandalwood. Musk or ambergris oils would be fantastic additions. Colorful blossoms, uva ursi, and linden leaves should be added to increase the beauty of the product.

FRUITY BASE VARIATIONS

Fragile Fruit (fruit & hay)

2 cups fruit base
2 cups heather flowers
2 cups woodruff
1 cup red clover blossoms
½ cup violet leaves
½ cup orris root

Very light fragrance that could be intensified with the addition of fruit oils and violet oil. Other floral oils would also be compatible. Tonka, vanilla, oak moss, linden leaves, spina cristi, and sumac berries would be nice additions. Malva, feverfew, globe amaranth, and more clover flowers would enhance the visual effect.

Faint Fruit (fruit & herb)

2 cups fruit base
2 cups yerba santa
2 cups southernwood
1 cup patchouli
1 cup angelica root

A just barely sweet, slightly fruity scent with a pungent element derived from the choice of herbs. Lavender, bay leaves, chamomile, allspice, orange peel, and related oils could be added. Spina cristi, rosehips, and uva ursi would be nice color and texture additives.

Flamboyant Fruit (fruit & menthol)

2 cups fruit base
2 cups peppermint
2 cups oak moss
1 cup lemon peel
1 cup orange peel
20 drops lime oil
10 drops strawberry oil

A sweet and sharp fragrance with real verve. Allspice, cinnamon, and cloves would add a nice spicy note. Change the look of this potpourri with uva ursi, spina cristi, rosehips, and flower blossoms. Experiment with additional fruit and citrus oils.

Fabled Fruit (fruit & resin)

2 cups fruit base
2 cups spina cristi
1 cup linden leaves
1 cup uva ursi

1 cup benzoin gum
½ cup frankincense
½ cup myrrh gum

A pleasing balsamic scent with a citrus and fruity element. All resinous formulas are also suitable for incense bases. Experiment with floral oils, musk, ambergris, ambrette seed, tonka, and sandalwood. Rosebuds and other blossoms could be added for more color.

Fancy Fruit (fruit & spice)

2 cups fruit base
2 cups blueberry leaf
1 cup allspice
1 cup coriander seed
1 cup cinnamon chips
½ cup nutmeg

½ cup orris root
10 drops each:
   allspice and
   tangerine oil
6 drops heliotrope oil
5 drops mace oil

A light, sweet, spicy fragrance reminiscent of fruitcake. Star anise and cloves would intensify the effect, and vanilla would make a nice addition. Calamus root or angelica root could be substituted for the orris root. Rosehips, uva ursi, and hibiscus flowers would be appropriate color and texture additions. Also try orange and lemon peel, spina cristi, tonka, and chamomile.

HAY-SCENTED BASE VARIATIONS

Halcyon Hay (hay & herb)

2 cups hay base
3 cups lavender flowers
2 cups bay leaves

½ cup sage
½ cup angelica root

Hay scents harmonize wonderfully with all other fragrances, but are really special when combined with lavender. This blend features a sweetened, softened lavender that is very pleasing. Judicious additions of sandalwood, lemon and orange peel, woodruff, tonka, vanilla, violet, lily-of-the-valley, and rose oil might sharpen this fragrance still further. Rosebuds, oak moss, feverfew, and malva flowers would add color and additional fragrance.

Hazy Hay (hay & menthol)

2 cups hay base
2 cups wintergreen
2 cups catnip

1½ cups pennyroyal
½ cup vetiver root

A soft, hazy edge-of-the-meadow-in-late-afternoon scent. Alter it with allspice, balm of Gilead buds, tonka, and oak moss. Add flower blossoms, linden, and uva ursi leaves for visual appeal.

Hosanna Hay (hay & resin)

2 cups hay base
1 cup orange blossoms
1 cup linden leaves
1 cup balm of Gilead buds

1 cup sandalwood
1 cup tonka beans
1 cup benzoin gum

This soft fragrance is the perfect base for rose oil and rosebuds. Experiment with other floral oils also. Add yarrow, feverfew, clover, and other flowers for color and texture.

Honey Hay (hay & spice)

2 cups hay base
2 cups allspice
1 cup cardamom pods

1 cup fennel seed
1½ cups cinnamon chips
½ cup oak moss

A very sweet, slightly licorice-scented blend. Add cloves or star anise to intensify the spiciness, or use allspice and cinnamon oil. Increase the oak moss, add tonka, balm of Gilead buds, and sandalwood. Blossoms and leaves should be added for appearance.

Heartwood Hay (hay & wood)

2 cups hay base
3 cups sandalwood

2 cups vetiver root
1 cup cedarwood chips

Hay and wood scents blend very well. To add a little more excitement to this fragrance, add floral oils and blossoms, tonka, balm of Gilead buds, lavender, citrus peels, oak moss, and vanilla.

HERB BASE VARIATIONS

High-Spirited Herbal (herbal & menthol)

2 cups herb base
3½ cups eucalyptus
1 cup cloves
1 cup juniper berries
½ cup calamus root

10 drops each:
cajeput,
rosemary, fir,
juniper, and
tarragon oils

A pungent, aromatic odor of light intensity. Increase the oils and add eucalyptus and clove oil to develop the intensity. Bay and lavender would be good additions. Add leaves, spices, and blossoms for more texture.

Hallelujah Herbal (herb & resin)

2 cups herb base
1½ cups frankincense
1½ cups myrrh gum
1 cup patchouli

1 cup lavender flowers
½ cup mace
½ cup ginger root

An aromatic, resinous fragrance that is suitable for the addition of floral oils or for burning as incense. Herbal oils and herbs such as sage, bay, and rose geranium would also be compatible. Spina cristi, blue malva, heather, calcatrippae, and orange flowers would add pleasing color and light fragrance.

Heartfelt Herbal (herb & spice)

2 cups herb base
2 cups ginger root
1 cup cinnamon chips
1 cup mace

1 cup star anise
½ cup nutmeg
½ cup angelica root
10 drops allspice oil

A dry and aromatic scent that could be sweetened with tonka, vanilla, or oak moss. Increase the dryness and pungency with white thyme oil or bay and other herbs. Uva ursi or linden leaves, broom flowers, tilia star flowers, and feverfew would add to the visual effect.

Hellacious Herbal (herb & wood)

2 cups herb base
3 cups cedar chips
1 cup lavender flowers
1 cup oak moss
½ cup wormwood
½ cup southernwood

20 drops each:
  lavender,
  patchouli, and
  rosemary oil
10 drops each:
  cedarwood, clove,
  and vetiver oil

The title of this potpourri refers to the moth repellent properties of the ingredients, and not to the fragrance itself. It has an aromatic cedarwood fragrance softened by the oak moss. Add feverfew flowers, tansy, and pennyroyal for their repellent properties.

Harmonizing Herbal (herb & musk)

2 cups herb base
2 cups marjoram
2 cups lavender flowers
1 cup Canada snake root

½ cup basil
½ cup orris root
25 drops musk oil

Musk works magic with all types of fragrances, but is especially softening and flattering with lavender and orris. This sweet scent would be suitable as the base of any floral or rose type potpourri. Benzoin, oak moss, and vanilla would be good additions. Use rosebuds, orange blossoms, or any other type of flower for color and texture.

MENTHOL BASE VARIATIONS

Mystical Menthol (menthol & resin)

2 cups menthol base
2 cups oak moss
2 cups orange peel

1 cup spearmint
1 cup benzoin gum

A sweet, resinous fragrance with a spearmint note. Frankincense, myrrh, lemon peel, tangerine, and lime oils would make interesting additions. Roses and other flowers could be added for color.

Melange Menthol (menthol & spice)

2 cups menthol base
2 cups cinnamon chips
1 cup allspice
1 cup pennyroyal

½ cup star anise
½ cup angelica root
1 cup cloves
10 drops anise oil

An aromatic spice mixture with an undertone of mint. Almost smells good enough to eat! Citrus and fruit oils and citrus peels would be good additions. Pine cones, tilia star flowers, linden and uva ursi leaves would be good textural additions.

Mercurial Menthol (menthol & wood)

2 cups menthol base
2 cups cedarwood chips
2 cups sandalwood
1 cup birch bark
1 cup vetiver root
1 tsp. thuja cedar leaf oil
½ tsp. sandalwood oil
¼ tsp. spruce oil

The evergreen effect of this blend is a good start toward the creation of a Christmas potpourri. Soften the sharpness with musk, and add spices or spice oils, citrus peels and oils, vanilla, or tonka. Hibiscus, safflower, poppy flowers, and red rosebuds would add touches of color. Pine cones and rosemary are appropriate for textural interest. Do not forget the traditional frankincense and myrrh.

Mellifluous Menthol (menthol & musk)

2 cups menthol base
2 cups woodruff
2 cups Canada snake root
1 cup catnip
½ cup allspice
½ cup calamus root
1 vanilla bean cut into
   ¼" pieces
2 tsp. musk oil

A very soft fragrance with only a hint of mint. Substitute pennyroyal or peppermint for the catnip, or add them or their oils if you want to intensify the menthol effect. As is, it would be a very good base for floral oils. Add flowers and leaves to create a colorful effect.

Medley Menthol (menthol & citrus)

2 cups menthol base
2 cups lemon peel
2 cups orange peel
1 cup spina cristi
½ cup coriander seed
½ cup orris root
1 tsp. each: orange
   and tangerine oils
15 drops pennyroyal oil

This combination produces rather a tart, but pleasing, fragrance. Combine with lavender, bay, rosemary, or other herbs. Experiment with different citrus oils. Uva ursi, spina cristi, linden leaves, and kesu flowers are suitable color and texture additives.

RESIN BASE VARIATIONS

Rococo Resin (resin & spice)

2 cups resin base
1 cup mace
1 cup cloves
1 cup cinnamon
1 cup ginger root

1 cup anise seed
½ cup allspice
½ cup frankincense
10 drops mace oil

A low, dry, somewhat softened spice fragrance that is deep and elaborate. Sweeten with tonka, vanilla, oak moss, and woodruff. Sandalwood and musk oil could be added, and also benzoin. Finish off with flower blossoms and leaves for color and texture.

Reknown Resin (resin & wood)

2 cups resin base
2 cups sandalwood
2 cups balm of Gilead buds
1 cup patchouli

1 cup oak moss
1 tsp. sandalwood oil
1 tsp. patchouli oil

An old-fashioned fragrance with a very dry, somewhat pungent note. More oak moss, tonka, and benzoin could be added. Lavender and rosebuds would also be nice additions.

Romantic Resin (resin & musk)

2 cups resin base
2 cups rosebuds
1½ cups woodruff
1 cup orange blossoms

1 cup oak moss
½ cup orris root
½ tsp. musk oil

Musk combines nicely with resins to create a soft and sweet fragrance suitable for the addition of floral oils. This would also be a good incense base. Try adding lily-of-the-valley or violet oil, vanilla, myrrh gum, tonka, and balm of Gilead buds.

Refreshing Resin (resin & citrus)

2 cups resin base
2 cups lemon peel
2 cups lemon balm
1 cup lemon verbena

½ cup orange peel
½ cup tonka
1 tsp. lime oil
1 tsp. bergamot oil

A dry and citrusy fragrance very suitable for experimentation with herbal and floral oils. Try adding lavender, roses, kesu, spina cristi, or spices to create a different effect.

Rose Resin (resin & floral)

2 cups resin base
2 cups rosebuds
2 cups orange blossoms
1 cup heather flowers

½ cup woodruff
½ cup orris root
1 tsp. lily-of-the-valley oil
1 tsp. rose oil

A sweet floral fragrance that is adaptable to many other additions. Try adding allspice, cloves, vanilla beans, orange blossoms, sandalwood, orris root, clover blossoms, lavender flowers, angelica, and more woodruff. Carnation, jasmine, violet, and rose geranium oils can be used to vary the effect. If you like floral blends this is a very good base to experiment with.

SPICE BASE VARIATIONS

Sassy Spice (spice & wood)

2 cups spice base
3 cups sassafras root
2 cups cedarwood chips

½ cup calamus root
½ cup vetiver root

A dry, spicy fragrance with a predominant sassafras note which will blend nicely with cloves, allspice, cinnamon, vanilla, and oak moss. Add uva ursi leaves, pink roses, and other materials for color and texture.

Sweet Spice (spice & musk)

2 cups spice base
2 cups woodruff
1 cup cinnamon chips
1 cup cloves

1 cup Canada snake root
1 cup oak moss
1 tsp. musk oil

A very sweet and spicy fragrance that would be compatible with lavender, myrrh, and tangerine oil. Flowers and leaves should be added for textural interest and colorful effect.

Subtle Spice (spice & citrus)

2 cups spice base
2 cups spina cristi
1½ cups lemon balm
1 cup orange peel

1 cup lemon peel
½ cup calamus root
1 tsp. grapefruit oil
1 tsp. sweet orange oil

A very delicate fragrance. Experiment with the addition of floral oils, sandalwood, and vanilla. Yarrow and uva ursi would add texture.

Seraphic Spice (spice & floral)

2 cups spice base
2 cups pink rosebuds
1½ cups red rosebuds
1 cup woodruff

½ cup allspice
½ cup cloves
½ cup orris root
1 tsp. carnation oil

Carnation is very compatible with spices. You may want to add other sweet florals such as honeysuckle, gardenia, or jasmine. Vanilla, sandalwood, tonka, oak moss, and musk would also make good additions.

Serenity Spice (spice & fruit)

2 cups spice base
3 cups chamomile
2 cups blackberry leaf
½ cup juniper berries

½ cup angelica root
25 drops strawberry oil
25 drops tangerine oil

This is a sweet and subtle fragrance. Try adding lavender, lemon balm, lemongrass, and lime oil. Spina cristi and uva ursi would sharpen the color and texture.

WOODY BASE VARIATIONS

Winsome Wood (wood & musk)

2 cups wood base
2 cups sassafras root
2 cups sarsaparilla root

2 cups vetiver
2 tsp. musk oil

This is an "outdoors" fragrance. Try adding evergreen oils; they are surprisingly nice with musk. Bay, uva ursi, linden leaves, white globe amaranth, yarrow flowers, and feverfew would make good decorative touches.

Wild Wood (wood & citrus)

2 cups wood base
2 cups lemon peel
2 cups orange peel
1 cup lemon verbena
½ cup lemon balm

½ cup calamus root
1 tsp. each: lemon,
   citronella, and
   bergamot oils

Citronella is the predominant scent. Add other citrus oils, particularly tangerine, ginger, rosemary, bay, and hibiscus flowers. Spina cristi, uva ursi, and pine cones would add color and texture.

Wistful Wood (wood & floral)

2 cups wood base
2 cups orange blossoms
2 cups woodruff
1½ cups heather flowers
½ cup orris root
1 tsp. gardenia oil
1 tsp. ylang ylang oil

A sweet floral that would be improved by the addition of allspice, vanilla, and deer's tongue leaves. Rosebuds, jasmine, and lavender should be added for extra fragrance, color, and texture.

Wondrous Wood (wood & fruit)

2 cups wood base
2 cups oak moss
1 cup raspberry leaf
1 cup blackberry leaf
1 cup blueberry leaf
1 cup chamomile
1 tsp. heliotrope oil
1 tsp. strawberry oil

A sweet fragrance of a delicately fruity nature. Try additional fruit or floral oils, and spina cristi, kesu flowers, clover blossoms, and woodruff for fragrance and texture.

Whimsical Wood (wood & hay)

2 cups wood base
2 cups woodruff
1½ cups linden leaves
1 cup red clover blossoms
1 cup violet leaves
¼ cup angelica root
¼ cup orris root
1½ tsps. violet oil
1½ tsps. lily-of-the-valley oil

A subtle and delicate fragrance that is blendable with herbs and florals. Try adding lemon balm, oak moss, myrrh gum, rosebuds, heather, orange peel, lemon peel, and tangerine oil.

FRAGRANT CRAFTS and GIFTS

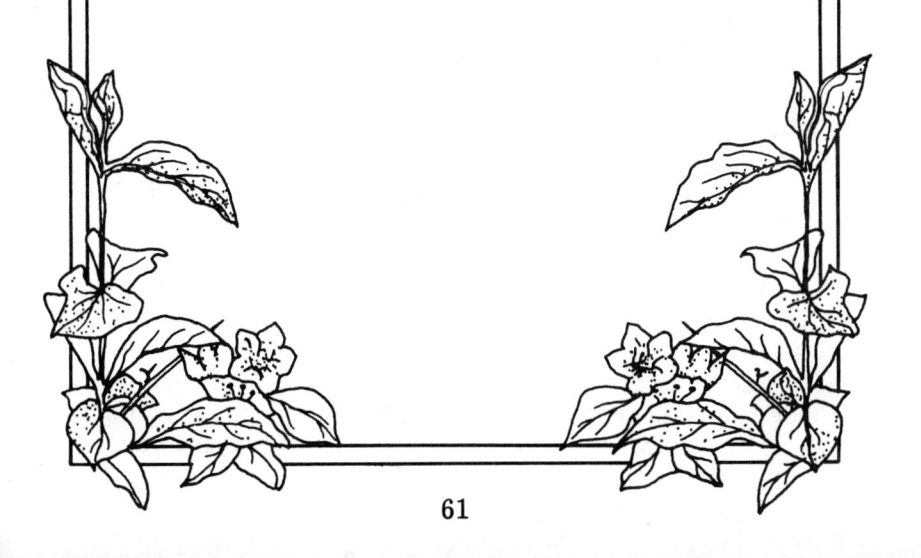

Showing Off Your Potpourri

Displaying your finished product is part of the fun in potpourri crafting. Dry-method potpourris retain the lovely, delicate colors of the original plant materials and are excellent for open-container displays. Show off your creations in baskets, bowls, jars, bottles, vases, and shells. A scavenger hunt around the house will result in all sorts of possible display containers.

Bring new life to your kitchen by packaging a spicy potpourri in a tea tin or canning jar. Conch and scallop shells are attractive containers and will brighten your bathroom. You can add a winning touch to your dining room by placing color-coordinated potpourri baskets on the buffet. A large ceramic bowl filled with potpourri and placed on the coffee table will become an instant conversation piece. Try baskets on bedside tables or decorate your desk with potpourri in jars.

Customizing potpourri displays and coordinating them with your furnishings can be exciting. Handmade lace and doilies bring beauty to any potpourri basket. Use the doily as a basket lining and the lace to create a delicate scalloped edge. Narrow ribbon, either woven through the lace or wrapped around the basket handle and tied in a bow, becomes a charming touch. Colors that match the predominant tints of the potpourri will help bring out the colors in your blend.

Layering materials in color bands is an interesting technique for clear glass jar displays. Imagine filling a jar with lavender, then heather flowers, pink rosebuds, red rosebuds, and a layer of potpourri made from all these materials. Experiment and vary the thickness of the layers to find the most visually appealing and personalized display.

You can create wonderful and unique gifts with your potpourri blends and displays. Baskets incorporating miniature figurines into tiny vignettes make excellent gifts. You can create your own orchestra by arranging tiny wooden angels with musical instruments on a cloud of silvery oak moss centered over a potpourri, or you can make a bird's nest from a grapevine basket with shredded vetiver mounding the rim. The rest of the basket can be filled with a mixture of rosemary, thyme, vetiver, cloves, patchouli, and peppermint. Speckled onyx eggs will make your nest complete. Baskets are fragile and can be damaged by wrapping, so if you are making gift baskets, just add a colorful ribbon and the present will be perfect.

Another gift idea is a potpourri-filled vase and silk flower arrangement. Anyone who smells the flowers will discover a wonderful potpourri fragrance. When you give a gift of clothing, make it extra special by adding sachet to the box or sprinkling sweet woodruff and rosebuds beneath the tissue paper.

Potpourri is so appealing you may be inclined to use it everywhere, but this can be expensive since it would take from fifty to one hundred pounds to scent an entire house. Potpourri in these amounts would cause odor fatigue, and you will only notice the fragrance when first entering the house. There are better, less expensive ways to scent your home.

To give your furniture a pleasant fragrance, tuck small sachets into the couch or chair cushions. You can also sprinkle woodruff, deer's tongue leaves, lemon balm, pennyroyal, chamomile, or rosebuds beneath cushions. You can even freshen mattresses by using these materials. The best way to freshen and scent furniture is to leave the materials in place for a few weeks before vacuuming.

A blend of spices and

Calendula
Calendula officinalis

herbs, or just herbs, mixed with baking soda makes a sensational rug deodorant. After sprinkling the mixture on the rug, let it stand a few hours before you vacuum. It is best to test the mixture on a hidden area, especially if you are using it on a light-colored rug.

Incense is another inexpensive way to add sweet scents to your surroundings, and it can be blended from many powdered botanicals (please refer to the chapter on incense). Sandalwood, cedarwood chips, frankincense, myrrh, and benzoin are great for the fireplace. Fragrant blends of spices, herbs, and oils placed in a pan of water on your stove will not only scent the air, they will also provide humidity to your home.

For a touch of romance, perfume the fuel in your oil lamp. Your imagination and perfume blends are all you need to discover new ways to add fragrance and pleasure to your home.

Sachets and Pastilles

Drawers and linen cabinets are great places for sachets and pastilles. Both of these mixtures will scent clothing and repel insects.

Sachets (small sacks of powdered potpourri materials) can be made from any formula in this book. The color and texture additives are not needed. Your blend is aged for two weeks, then ground in a blender or coffee mill, and placed into sachet cases. Working with materials that have already been powdered gives a more accurate idea of the final scent.

To make an easy sachet mixture, combine an equal amount of powdered fixative with a neutral material such as arrowroot starch or sawdust. Orris root powder is a popular fixative for a sachet. Essential oils can be added next, in any combination you like. Transfer the blend to a sachet case with a funnel.

The base blend system, varied by adding different materials or oils, can also be used to make a sachet. A nice blend can be made from one pound of orris root combined with one pound of sandalwood, four ounces each of lavender, vetiver, ambrette seed, and cedarwood; six ounces each of woodruff and patchouli, two ounces of both tonka and benzoin, and one-half ounce of musk oil. You can experiment and make variations of this sweet, neutral fragrance. One variation can be made by adding two ounces of each of the following: balm of Gilead buds, cloves, cinnamon, allspice, and tonka, and one ounce of both cardamom and myrrh.

Remember when you are experimenting to work in small quantities. Work with teaspoon-sized amounts, and limit yourself to no more than eight materials in combinations. Begin with equal portions of each material and then adjust them if you need to, but keep in mind that fifty percent fixative is needed to help retain the sachet's fragrance.

Some combinations you may want to try in your experiments with sachet are presented in Figure 1.

Figure 1

Combination	Materials Used
1	lavender, rose, woodruff, orris, orange blossoms, tonka, sandalwood
2	orris, sandalwood, violet oil, orange blossoms, vanilla
3	patchouli, oak moss, cedar, benzoin
4	musk oil, sandalwood, benzoin, tonka, myrrh
5	rosemary, peppermint, cloves, thyme, vetiver, southernwood
6	lavender, rosemary, sage, bay, angelica
7	lemon balm, lemon peel, lemon verbena, lemon and other citrus oils, orris
8	oak moss, balm of Gilead, sandalwood, orris, tonka, floral oils
9	cedarwood, southernwood, wormwood, patchouli, oak moss, vetiver, lavender, cloves, pennyroyal
10	allspice, cinnamon, vanilla, calamus, carnation oil
11	rose, clover, woodruff, violet leaves, deer's tongue leaves, tonka, oak moss

An interesting approach to sachet blending is to create "his and hers" mixtures. Make up a quantity of base including materials you both like, then divide the base and individualize the fragrance of each part with oils.

It is also easy to customize a sachet base with subtle

variations. Each variation can be useful for different types of clothing. Musk and jasmine are sensual, and when added to the sachet blend, are suitable for lingerie. Insect-repellent materials can be added to sachets for use in storage closets. Oak moss is a sweet-smelling, guaranteed moth-proofer. Rue, savory, chamomile, and especially pennyroyal, are repugnant to fleas. Flies can be repelled by using clover flowers, sassafras, clove, bay, eucalyptus, and tansy. Mosquitoes hate citronella and citrus oils. Other materials which will discourage insects are: feverfew, mint, bergamot, lavender, tonka, patchouli, vetiver, sandalwood, woodruff, calamus, cedarwood, southernwood, wormwood, and pine oils. Avoid using the oils from phlox, mignonette, primrose, or other night-blooming flowers, because they attract moths.

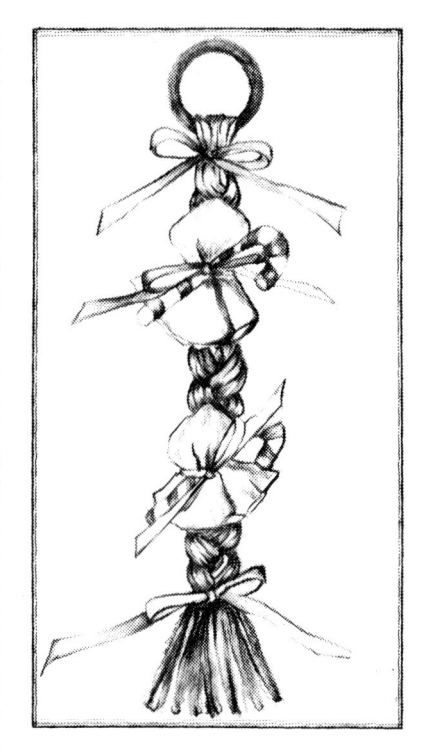

Sachets, whether created for fragrance or as moth repellents, need to be put into cases. These can be simple or elaborate, but finely woven silk works best, because it prevents powders from leaking out. If you want to use needlework or loosely woven fabric as a sachet case, you will also need an inner liner.

Heart-shaped, quilted red satin, or fabrics cut into circles, ovals, diamonds, triangles, or squares that have been trimmed with laces, ribbons, or sequins make attractive sachet cases. Finish the case by adding a ribbon loop, so it can be suspended from door knobs or clothes hangers. Large flat sachets scent blankets stored on closet shelves.

Even if you do not sew, you can make sachets. One way to create a sachet is to seal the mixture in envelopes and place them in drawers. You can make your own decorative envelopes from wrapping paper or origami paper. Another simple method for non-sewers is the "ball of sachet" method. Cut squares or circles of fabric with pinking shears. Place a small mound of sachet in the center, then gather the fabric edges and hold in place with rubber bands. Make a bow around the rubber bands with ribbon to complete the case. Embroidered or appliqued handkerchiefs with pre-finished edges also make good cases. They look fancy, but are simple to make.

Pastilles are tiny tablets made of ground materials, oils, and a binding agent. They are the easiest way to scent drawers and shelves. Pastilles can be made by several methods. Each of these techniques will produce several dozen pastilles in only an hour.

Wax pastilles can be made by following the same techniques used in candle-making. You will need paraffin or beeswax, candy molds or miniature cupcake tins, and a recycled tin can to use as an improvised double boiler. If you have any trouble finding a mold, you can use a shoebox lined with greased aluminum foil, and cut the wax into smaller pieces with a sharp knife after it is cool.

Since wax ignites easily, always melt it in the can placed in a pot of boiling water—never directly over the flame. When the wax is melted, add small shavings of candle color and stir with a dowel rod or stick until it dissolves completely and evenly into the wax. Next, essential oils can be added, a drop at a time, until the desired fragrance is reached. Stir the wax well, remove it from the stove, and pour it into molds greased with vegetable shortening. Remove the pastilles from the molds after they have cooled.

Children love homemade play dough that has been scented with oils. The homemade version works just like regular play dough; it can be molded or shaped and allowed to dry to make pastilles. To make homemade play dough, mix two and one-quarter cups white flour (not self-rising) with one cup salt and one tablespoon alum. Add four tablespoons essential oil to the dry mixture and stir in one and one-half cups boiling water. Use a mixer to stir the dough and add food coloring if you want colored dough.

A more artistic dough can be made by mixing together one cup of gum tragacanth and one cup powdered fixative. Add whatever essential oils you desire and blend in one cup of lukewarm water. Mix this well and add more water—never more than two cups—if necessary. Knead the dough by hand until it resembles pie or bread dough. Run the mixture through a cookie press or hand shape it to make pastilles. The pastilles should be allowed to air dry before you use them.

Fragrant Ornaments for Any Season

Pomanders are spicy, sweetly scented decorations made from fruits that are thick-skinned, firm, and unblemished. Fruits that work well for this are apples, oranges, limes, lemons, tangerines, or kumquats.

A wooden skewer or chopstick can be used to pierce the fruit from stem end to blossom end. The stick needs to be left in place until the pomander is completely dried. This will leave a channel through the center of your pomander through which you can attach a ribbon for hanging the ornament.

Pierce small holes in the skin of the fruit with pointed tweezers and push whole cloves into the fruit. Decorative effects can be created by patterning the cloves in stripes, swirls, or stars, covering as much of the surface as possible. Pomanders with an evenly studded pattern are usually the best. Open areas of skin, which expand and contract at different rates when the fruit is drying, may develop bumps and cracks.

After studding the fruit with cloves, roll it in a mixture of powdered spices and fixatives. Keep the spices or powdered botanicals you select in a fifty-fifty ratio to the fixative. You can enhance the fragrance of the spice mixture by adding different oils. Apply sweet orange oil, or other oils, to the exposed skin with an eyedropper so the spice mixture will adhere to the fruit. Gently shake the fruit and spice mixture in a small paper or plastic bag. The pomander then needs to be stored in a cool dry place for several weeks to dry completely. However, if you are in a hurry to use the pomander, it can be dried in an oven for several hours at the lowest temperature setting. This drying method will give the pomander a cooked odor.

The spices, herbs, and fixatives you use in the rolling mixture will vary the color of your pomanders. Red sandalwood and rosewood produce a reddish color. Bay will add a light greenish-yellow to the pomander. You can alter the color and texture of the ornament by applying perfect whole star anise to the surface in patterns along with the cloves. Hold the stars in place with glass-headed pins. For a glittering effect, attach sequins and beads to the pomander when you apply the cloves. After the pomander is dry, thread color-coordinated ribbons through the center channel to make hanging loops.

Pomanders can be placed in closets to impart sweet scents to your clothes. Try hanging a "spicy" pomander in your kitchen, or a "citrusy" one in the bathroom.

One sweet, rich fragrance mixture for rolling pomanders is made of allspice, cinnamon, clove, orris, musk oil, and sandalwood oil. Other combinations you may want to use with pomanders are:

* orris and sandalwood with lavender oil
* coriander, allspice, calamus, and tangerine oil
* tonka, cloves, vanilla, and musk oil
* rosemary, angelica, bay, and pennyroyal
* anise, licorice, cinnamon, tonka, oak moss, and cinnamon oil
* frankincense, myrrh, sandalwood, and musk oil

At Christmas, display your pomanders in a bowl or basket with tree ornaments that shine and contrast. Smaller pomanders—made of lemons, limes, and tangerines—are usually light enough after they have dried to hang on a tree. Tiny kumquats can be strung on florist's wire and shaped into scented wreaths and garlands.

Scented Christmas tree ornaments can be created in several other imaginative ways. Small cornucopias, baskets or boxes folded from wrapping paper can be used to hold fragrant potpourri. Hang sachets from the tree or make them into holiday mobiles. Shape or mold scented playdough into ornaments, or roll them out and cut fragrant gingerbread men.

Pine cone ornaments can be used like pomanders. They are simpler and faster to make. Dip the cone into white glue and then into a pomander rolling mixture. Allow this to dry before painting white glue on the upper tips. Dredge them in clear glitter ("diamond dust") for a frosted snow look. Glue a pearl bead to the top of each cone and attach a gold thread to hang your ornament. You can also string miniature pine cones for garlands. These fragrant pine cone decorations will give your tree a truly natural look.

Traditionally, Christmas is the time for ornaments, but with a few alterations you can make ornaments appropriate for other seasons as well.

Create Perfumes and Colognes

If you like fragrance, perfume making can be a rewarding and fascinating hobby. It is also inexpensive. Commercial perfumes can cost as much as $250 per ounce, but you can make a gallon of your own perfume for much less. A $50 investment will enable you to create a wide range of perfumes, colognes, and toilet waters.

The ratio of essential oils to alcohol makes the difference in perfume, cologne, and toilet water. Perfume has the highest ratio—20 percent and up, while toilet water has the lowest ratio—from two to five percent. The ratio for cologne can range from five to twelve percent. There is no government regulation concerning the exact proportions, and manufacturers determine their own product standards.

The equipment you will need—eyedroppers, one-dram to four-ounce bottles, measuring spoons and cups, filter paper—is relatively inexpensive. Muslin is the best filter paper, but if unavailable, coffee filters or several layers of good-quality paper towels can be substituted. The materials required to make perfume include essential oils—both natural and synthetic—dried botanicals, and 190-proof grain alcohol (which is available at liquor stores in one-fifth bottles).

Certain substances are not available as oils or in oil form, and an alcohol extract must be made from the dry material. To make an

Tea Rose
Rosa odorata

alcohol extract, soak one part powdered or chopped material in six parts alcohol. Measure the materials by volume and place in a closed container. Stir or shake the container every day for seven to ten days, then remove the "perfume" from the container and pour it through filter paper or pure talc. Add more pure alcohol to bring the quantity back to the original amount used. This produces an extract or perfume which can be used as is or blended with additional oils or extracts.

Perfumes must contain a fixative in a ratio of 15 percent in order to retain their scent. Angelica, calamus, orris, vetiver, and musk are all available in the oil form and are excellent perfume fixatives. If you cannot obtain fixatives in the oil form, an alcohol extract can be made from the dry material (as previously described). Ideally, the fixative is combined with the oil or extract as you go along, since it lends a scent of its own. However, there is no harm done if you add the fixative as the final step.

Experiment with combinations of two to six different essential oils, fragrance oils, or extracts. Limiting the number of components will minimize confusion. A drop of each oil will be enough until you are familiar with the interactions of the oils. Take careful notes of your experiments and your reactions to them. When you have a fragrance you like, dilute it with alcohol, using the proportions necessary for the desired perfume-or cologne-strength solution. Small amounts of distilled water will cut the odor of alcohol. Next a fixative oil is required in a ratio of 15 percent. Pour the perfume into a bottle, carefully seal it, and store the bottle in a cool, dark place for two to four weeks to age.

Now you will be able to use a perfume as unique as you are!

The Complete Bathing Experience

Nothing is more relaxing than a soothing herbal bath, and because it is inexpensive, the pleasure is doubled. Bath salts, herbal blends, and facial-steaming mixtures are easy to make. Homemade products such as scented witch hazel, cosmetic vinegars, dusting powders, massage oils, and bath oils are affordable luxuries.

Massage and bath oils are made by adding essential oils to carrier oils. Castor, sweet almond, and apricot kernel oils can be used alone or in combination; they work best for dry to normal skin. Olive, cocoa butter, and palm oil are also good for this skin type. If you have normal to oily skin, you may want to use oils with a semi-drying effect, such as corn, sesame, and sunflower oils. Start with a few drops of essential oil to one tablespoon of carrier oil. Depending on individual taste, you can increase the essential oil up to one teaspoon. Generally speaking, more fragrance is required for bath oils since they will be diluted in water. A recloseable plastic squeeze bottle is convenient to store your mixture. The fragrance will fade in time, so it is best to only blend a one-month supply.

Bath salts are made from common and inexpensive materials. They consist of various combinations of fragrance, salt (sodium chloride), borax (sodium borate), washing soda (sodium carbonate), and baking soda (sodium bicarbonate). Sometimes boric and tartaric acids are also added. All of these ingredients can be purchased at any food or drug store.

Any blend of these materials is pleasing. Try mixing one part baking soda to two parts salt, or equal amounts of borax and washing soda. You may even want to combine all four ingredients in equal quantities. Stir the mixture, add essential oils, then store it in sealed jars or tins. A few tablespoons per bath will bring increased pleasure to bathing. You may want to be extravagant and use a whole cup!

You can make an effervescent bath by combining ten parts cream of tartar with nine parts baking soda, six parts

Hop Plant
Humulus lupulus

rice flour or arrowroot starch, and one part essential oil. A blender is a helpful tool to disperse the oil evenly throughout the powders. A glass, water-proof container preserves your concoction until you are ready to add ½ cup to your bath.

Create an enjoyable bubble bath by combining 12 parts soap flakes with 16 parts hot water. In another container, dissolve one-eighth part essential oils in one part alcohol and two parts glycerin. Combine these two mixtures and store the bubble bath in a wide-mouth jar.

Sensitive or irritated skin can be soothed in an emollient bath. These baths can be made by soaking finely ground bran, oatmeal, or barley in warm water and then straining the mixture. Add the water to the bath along with soothing oils (up to one teaspoon) such as chamomile or lavender. You can use any one of the grains, or combine them in the proportion of one pound of grain to two quarts of water. Almond meal or skim milk powder can also be used in smaller quantities in the bath. (This recipe is not recommended for storage.)

Herbal blends will add fragrance and other qualities to your bath water. These solutions can be combined with any of the bath mixtures that have already been explained, or they can be used alone. There are an amazing number of herbs that can be used in facial steams and bath blends. Many of these herbs are shown in Figure 2. Different herbs produce different results. If you have a specific effect in mind, consult an herbal book or a book on aromatherapy to see which herb will produce the outcome you desire.

Figure 2

agrimony	eucalyptus	lovage
alfalfa	feverfew	malva leaf
bay	fennel	marigold
birch bark	fo-ti-tieng	(calendula)
borage	geranium leaves	mugwort
burdock	ginger	oak moss
burnet	hops	pansy
chamomile	hyssop	passion flower
clary sage	jasmine	patchouli
clover	juniper	peach leaves
comfrey	kelp	raspberry leaves
dandelion	lemon balm	rosemary
dill	lemon thyme	roses
echinacea	linden	savory
elder flowers	licorice	

A facial steam opens the pores and cleanses the skin. Certain herbs also contribute beneficial effects. To make a facial steam, simply place the herbs (one cup) with a quart of water in a glass or stainless steel pan. Bring to a boil and turn it off. Next drape a towel over your head and place your face over the pan, trying to capture all the steam. When you have finished, your skin will feel revitalized and healthy.

Steeping herbs for about 15 minutes in boiling water or vinegar is the best way to prepare an herbal bath. Use approximately one cup of herbs to each quart of liquid. Strain the mixture and pour the liquid into your bath. If you have used water in the mixture, you can also use the liquid as a facial steam before pouring it into the bath.

Another way to make an herbal bath is to wrap herbs with an equal amount of borax in a handkerchief or cloth scrap. Securely fasten the fabric with a rubber band and hang it from the faucet while running hot water. Be careful that the cloth does not come apart, because the herbs may clog your drain. One way to avoid spilling the herbs is to make a drawstring sack of either silk or muslin. You can remove the herbs from your "bath sack" after each bath, rinse it with cold water, and reuse the sack.

Essential oils can be added to arrowroot starch, rice powder, cornstarch, or talc to make dusting powder. Place the dry ingredients in a blender, along with a few drops of oil, blend, and when the powders are settled, note the fragrance. If you wish, more oil can be added. Orris root is sometimes combined with the starches in quantities up to 25 percent. Orris is known as a fixative, but also imparts its own unique fragrance. (Some individuals are allergic to orris; please see Appendix V to perform a skin allergy test.)

One cup of vinegar or rubbing alcohol, three cups of distilled water, and a few drops (up to $\frac{1}{2}$ teaspoon) of a fragrant oil can be combined to make facial astringents and hair rinses. Gently pat them on after a facial steam to close the skin's pores, or use them as a final hair rinse after shampooing. Witch hazel extract can also be scented with oil and can act as an astringent.

From beginning to end, fragrance can add to the enjoyment of your beauty routine.

Incense

In addition to being the least expensive way to perfume your home, incense can be used to scent clothing, paper, and books. Incense is an easy-to-make combination of powdered resins, spices, and woods that can be burned on unscented charcoal briquettes.

Incense charcoal, available in stores selling religious materials, is treated to ignite easily and burn steadily. These briquettes have a tendency to spark, so it is best to hold them with tweezers when lighting them. Place the charcoal on a china plate or some other heat-resistant surface and dust the powder evenly over the surface. You may need to dust the coals again later to guarantee a steady release of fragrance.

A simple recipe for incense powder is an equal proportion of frankincense and myrrh. You may want to experiment and add an equal amount of sandalwood or cinnamon. Let your own sense of smell be your guide.

Paper, clothing, and books can be scented by placing them above the incense brazier in a small room. If it is possible, carefully drape a blanket so the smoke is concentrated but oxygen can still reach the briquette. The charcoal will burn through in about an hour.

It is possible to make your own incense cones, but it can be a messy job. Grind high-quality wood charcoal and combine 12 parts charcoal to one part potassium nitrate (nitre or saltpeter). The potassium nitrate will readily ignite and burn evenly. Add up to 12 parts: powdered spices, resins, woods, and oils. Blend in two parts tragacanth gum, a binding agent, and slowly add water until the powder has a consistent dough-like texture. Shape the dough into cones and allow them to dry before burning them.

If incense is too strong for your taste and you find it is too much work to make it, you may want to scent candles instead. It is easy to make scented candles by following a standard candlemaking procedure and using essential oils for fragrance.

Fragrant Wreaths

Scented wreaths have been popular decorations for many years. Originally they were made of fresh materials that needed to be replaced often. Eventually bundles of dried herbs took the place of fresh materials. Culinary wreaths, used for seasoning, were never far from the cook's hand. Other herbs were fashioned into wreaths and placed on doors to keep witches and other "evils" away from the home.

You are probably not worried about witches, but a scented wreath can still make a handsome accessory for any door. You can make fragrant wreaths by using one of two wreath forms: one is a straw base, the other is a styrofoam base. Both of these types of wreaths are available from craft stores. In addition to the forms, you will need white glue or rubber cement, T-pins, glass-headed pins, ribbons, laces, tweezers, fine-gauge wire or florist's wire, grain alcohol, whole and powdered spices and herbs, dried flowers, and oils.

Before you even open your glue bottle, decide where you want the focal point to be on your wreath. The focal point is where your eyes will be drawn first when you look at the wreath. You can divide the circle in half, quarters, eighths, or sixteenths, either horizontally or vertically. Pattern segments can be repeated in each section. It does not matter if the design is balanced or uneven, but your eyes should find the focal point naturally, then travel around the remainder of the wreath. As you work on the pattern, check to see if it looks correct. If so, you have a design with the right balance of movement and stillness.

Cover the styrofoam wreath with white glue and let your imagination go as you place dried materials on it. Good materials for a scented wreath are: woodruff, mint, lemon balm, patchouli, heather, lavender, oak moss, and yerba santa. To give the wreath an overall effect of color, accent it with one material, such as lavender flowers. You may want to arrange materials in stripes or use a pre-mixed potpourri. Whole spices can be arranged in patterns and then glued into place. Tiny kumquat pomanders or citrus peel strips, small sachets, pastilles, decorated pine

Fragrant Cinnamon
Straw Wreath

cones or silk flowers complete the composition. Wrapping ribbons and bows around the form makes a charming finishing touch.

Straw wreaths are made a little differently. Dissolve any combination of fragrance or essential oils in alcohol and spray the wreath until it is saturated, then allow it to dry. Glue on spices, whole bay leaves, or other materials in patterns. String cinnamon sticks on florist's wire and zig-zag them around the form. Additional wire can be used to hold the sticks in place.

Vanilla beans, long cinnamon sticks, and licorice root pieces can be combined with silk flowers and foliage to make an attractive display. You may even want to pin sachet or potpourri wrapped in bridal netting to the wreath for an additional touch of fragrance. Circle the wreath with ribbons and lace, and pin it to the back with T-pins. Give a final touch to your creation by adding a colorful bow.

Wreaths can also make wonderful gifts. Match the ribbon and lace colors to those used in the receiver's home, or try making a wreath that has some practical value. Follow a theme. The tea drinker's wreath is made of tea bags, tiny bundles of tea herbs, and a tea strainer. For the cook, glue whole bay leaves around a styrofoam form in an overlapping scale pattern, attach whole garlic cloves, individualized bouquet garni (herbs and spices wrapped in cheesecloth), and use a ribbon to attach a garlic press. If the wreath has been carefully designed, it will still look good even after the food products have been removed. Be creative and design a special wreath for an incense-lover, bath sachet-user, or potpourri-crafter.

APPENDIXES

Appendix I
Quality and Effect Vocabulary

The Quality and Effect Vocabulary is a list of antonyms created to help you determine the overall effect of a blend or a raw material.

Simply run down the list and determine which of the paired words accurately describes the fragrance. Occasionally, neither word or both words may apply. Keep this list handy whenever you are formulating blends. Check it repeatedly in the course of product development. It takes little time to do and can be quite helpful.

Quality and Effect Vocabulary

sharp-dull
sweet-bitter
rich-poor
weak-strong
wet-dry
warm-cool
mellow-crude
pungent-bland
earthy-airy
pleasant-noxious
placid-animated
fragrant-malodorous
fresh-stale
aromatic-fetid
erotic-ingenuous
elusive-concrete

low-high
deep-shallow
dark-bright
sad-happy
soft-hard
faint-intense
ripe-raw
flat-piquant
potent-dilute
narcotic-stimulating
acid-alkaline
mild-harsh
aroused-subdued
soothing-exciting
redolent-rank
robust-feeble

Appendix II
Standard Units of Measurement
Volume

U.S. Liquid Measure	U.S. Equivalents	Metric Equivalents
fluid dram	60 minims, 0.2256 cubic inches	3.697 milliliters
fluid ounce	8 fluid drams, 1.8047 cubic inches	29.573 milliliters
cup	8 fluid ounces, 14.4375 cubic inches	.2365 liter
pint	2 cups, 28.875 cubic inches	.473 liter
quart	2 pints, 57.75 cubic inches	.946 liter
gallon	4 quarts, 231 cubic inches	3.785 liters

U.S. Dry Measure	U.S. Equivalents	Metric Equivalents
pint	0.5 quart, 33.6 cubic inches	.551 liter
quart	2 pints, 67.2 cubic inches	1.101 liters
peck	8 quarts, 537.605 cubic inches	8.810 liters

Weight

U.S. Customary Unit	U.S. Equivalents	Metric Equivalents
grain	.036 dram, .002285 ounce	64.79891 milligrams
dram	27.344 grains, .0625 ounce	1.772 grams
ounce	16 drams, 437.5 grains	28.350 grams
pound	16 ounces, 7,000 grains	453.59237 grams

HOUSEHOLD MEASURES - EQUIVALENTS

1 cup = 8 fluid ounces = 16 tablespoons
¾ cup = 12 tablespoons (6 fluid ounces)
⅔ cup = 10 tablespoons + 2 teaspoons
½ cup = 8 tablespoons (4 fluid ounces)
⅓ cup = 5 tablespoons + 1 teaspoon
¼ cup = 4 tablespoons (2 fluid ounces)
⅛ cup = 2 tablespoons (1 fluid ounce)
1 tablespoon = ½ fluid ounce (3 teaspoons)
1 teaspoon = 60 drops

Appendix III
Volume-to-Weight Chart

One Cup =	Weight in Ounces
Alfalfa leaf c/s	1.32
Allspice ground	4.05
Allspice whole	3.18
Angelica root c/s	3.34
Anise seed ground	3.58
Anise seed whole	3.48
Anise, star, ground	3.88
Anise, star, whole	2.22
Annatto seed whole	5.81
Arnica flowers whole	.75
Balm of Gilead buds whole	3.23
Basil leaf imported c/s	1.57
Bay leaf whole	.26
Bayberry bark c/s	3.09
Bayberry bark powder	4.03
Benzoin gum powder	4.01
Birch bark c/s	3.94
Blackberry leaf c/s	1.13
Blueberry leaf c/s	.61
Borage leaf c/s	1.10
Broom flowers whole	.74
Calamus root c/s	2.52
Calcatrippae flowers whole	.40
Calendula flowers whole	.90
Canada snakeroot c/s	3.07
Caraway seed ground	3.48
Caraway seed whole	3.95
Cardamom seed decort. ground	3.75
Cardamom seed decort. whole	5.88
Catnip herb c/s	1.52
Cedar chips, red	.62
Celery seed whole	4.11
Chamomile flowers whole	.76
Chicory root raw c/s	4.44

c/s   – cut and sifted
decort. – decorticated

Volume-to-Weight Chart (cont.)

One Cup =	Weight in Ounces
Cinnamon ground	4.26
Cinnamon chips cut	4.69
Clover tops, red	.59
Cloves ground	4.34
Cloves whole	3.42
Coriander seed ground	3.57
Coriander seed whole	2.94
Cornsilk c/s	.54
Cubeb berry whole	2.60
Cumin seed ground	4.26
Cumin seed whole	3.98
Dill seed whole	3.67
Elder berries whole	3.65
Elder flowers whole	1.68
Eucalyptus leaf c/s	1.99
Fennel seed ground	3.41
Fennel seed whole	2.82
Fenugreek seed whole	6.31
Feverfew flowers	.54
Frankincense tears	5.36
Frankincense powder	5.25
Ginger root c/s	4.19
Ginger root ground	3.78
Ginger root whole	3.70
Globe Amaranth flowers whole	.47
Hawthorn berries whole	3.97
Heather flowers whole	1.05
Hibiscus flowers whole	1.29
Hibiscus flowers whole Mexican	.98
Hop flowers (sweet) whole	.61
Hyssop herb c/s	1.45
Juniper berries whole	2.99
Kesu flowers whole	.67
Lavender flowers whole	1.01
Lemon balm leaf c/s	.69
Lemongrass c/s	1.40
Lemon peel c/s	3.01
Lemon peel granulated	4.43
Lemon thyme c/s	1.19
Lemon verbena leaf c/s	1.13
Licorice mint (anise hyssop)	1.14

Volume-to-Weight Chart (cont.)

One Cup =	Weight in Ounces
Licorice root c/s	3.01
Licorice sticks whole 8"	.39 ea. (avg.)
Life everlasting flowers whole	.54
Linden leaf & flower whole	.31
Mace "siftings"	3.22
Mace ground	4.51
Malva flowers whole, black	.44
Malva flowers whole, blue	.28
Myrrh gum c/s	5.02
Myrrh gum powder	5.46
Nutmeg ground	4.25
Nutmeg whole	6.02
Oak moss c/s	.29
Oat straw c/s	.89
Orange peel c/s	3.63
Orange peel granulated	2.81
Orange petals whole	.98
Orris root natural c/s	4.30
Orris root natural powder	4.09
Orris root peeled c/s	5.58
Passion flower herb c/s	1.53
Patchouli herb c/s	1.23
Pennyroyal herb c/s	1.13
Peppermint leaf c/s	1.54
Pine cones 3/4"	.59
Poppy flowers whole, red	.59
Raspberry leaf c/s	.86
Rosebuds and petals, pink	.79
Rosebuds and petals, red	.65
Rosehips seedless c/s	3.41
Rosehips whole	3.62
Rosemary leaf whole	1.09
Rue herb c/s	1.89
Safflower petals whole	.77
Sage leaf whole	.58
Sandalwood yellow chips	2.90
Sandalwood yellow powder	3.53
Sarsaparilla root c/s	2.18
Sassafras root bark c/s	2.17
Saw palmetto berries whole	4.15
Senna leaf whole	.68

Volume-to-Weight Chart (cont.)

One Cup =	Weight in Ounces
Southernwood herb c/s	1.96
Spearmint leaf c/s	1.46
Spina cristi whole	1.06
Strawberry leaf c/s	1.55
Sumac berries whole	3.58
Tansy herb c/s	2.03
Thyme leaf c/s	1.84
Tilia star flower whole	1.86
Tonka beans whole	4.13
Uva ursi leaf whole	1.64
Valerian root c/s	5.47
Vetiver root c/s	.94
Vetiver root powder	3.94
Violet leaf c/s	.78
White oak bark c/s	2.53
White pine bark c/s	2.34
White willow bark c/s	2.15
Wild cherry bark c/s	3.54
Wintergreen leaf c/s	1.90
Wood betony herb c/s	1.52
Woodruff herb c/s	1.15
Wormwood herb c/s	1.49
Yarrow flower whole	.30
Yerba santa leaf c/s	.71

Appendix IV
FDA Restricted Usage List

Arnica flowers
Balm of Gilead buds
Belladonna
Calamus root
Cedarwood and cedarwood oil
Galangal root
Heliotrope flowers and heliotrope oil
Lemon Verbena
Lily-of-the-valley flowers and lily-of-the-valley oil
Linden leaves and flowers
Lobelia
Mugwort
Musk oil
Myrtle
Oak moss
Pansy
Periwinkle
Saint John's Wort
Sassafrass root bark and sassafrass oil
Southernwood
Tansy
Thistle
Thuja cedar leaf oil
Tonka beans
Vervain, blue
Vetiver root and vetiver oil
Woodruff
Wormwood
Yarrow flowers

Appendix V
Skin Allergy Test

Even natural products can cause skin irritations for many people. Before using any product as an ingredient in bath sachet, dusting powder, perfumes or cologne, it is a good idea to try this simple allergy test.

If you are using a liquid product, dilute a small amount in water or alcohol and spread it on the inside of your forearm. Cover the area with an adhesive bandage and after 24 hours check for redness, swelling, rash, or other irritations.

With solids or powders, soak a small amount in water or alcohol to make a diluted solution and apply the same way you would a liquid product.

If you find that a product causes an irritation, discontinue using the material in your blends.

Appendix VI
Fragrance Vocabulary

Describing a fragrance is not easy. The sense of smell is subjective, and, to add to the problem, there are few words in the English language to describe fragrances. Think about it for a minute, then try to describe the aroma of a tangerine. You probably had to resort to comparisons. Maybe you said something like: "Tangy. Citrusy. Almost like an orange only different." If so, what does an orange smell like?

Perfumers have tried to relieve this problem with fragrance vocabularies. These lists, made up of well-known fragrances, natural products and raw fragrance materials, give the perfumer a way to characterize a new product or raw material by mentally comparing it to familiar smells. This can be done only when you are acquainted with the scents of all the items on the list. Consequently, becoming familiar with the fragrances listed in the following "Fragrance Vocabulary" will help you create new blends or analyze new materials.

Oriental Poppy
Papaver orientale

Fragrance Vocabulary

acacia	cigar	green
acidic	citronella	ham
alcohol	citrus	harsh
almondy	civet	hay
amber	clam	heather
ammonia	clean	heliotrope
animal	clove	herbal
anise	coconut	hickory smoke
antiseptic	cod liver oil	honey
apple	coffee	honeysuckle
apple blossom	cognac	hyacinth
apricot	cooked	icy
astringent	creosote	incense
bacon	cucumber	iris
baked	cumin	ivy
balsamic	curry	jam
banana	dill	jasmine
basil	disinfectant	juniper berry
beer	dry	jonquil
bitter	dry leaves	lavender
black currant	earthy	leafy
blue grass	ethereal	lemon
bread	fatty	lemongrass
broken twig	fecal	leathery
burned sugar	feet	licroice
burnt	fern	lighter fluid
butterscotch	fig	lilac
buttery	fish	lily
camphor	floral	lime
candy	frankincense	linseed
caramel	fresh	mace
carnation	fruity	malt
carrot	fuel oil	maple
cedar	gardenia	marigold
celery	garlic	meadow
chamomile	gasoline	meaty
cherry	gassy	medicinal
chocolate	geranium	melon
chrysanthemum	ginger	menthol
cinnamon	glue	metallic
cheese	grapefruit	milky
chemical	grass	mimosa
choking	greasy	minty

94

Fragrance Vocabulary (cont.)

mossy	plastic	sweet
mothballs	plant	tangerine
mushroom	plum	tar
musky	popcorn	tart
mustard	potatoe	tea
musty	powdery	thyme
myrrh	prune	tobacco
naptha	pungent	toffee
narcissus	rancid	tonka
new-mown hay	raspberry	tuberose
nutty	resinous	turpentine
nutmeg	rhubarb	tutti fruiti
oak moss	roasted	urine
oatmeal	root beer	valerian
oily	rooty	vanilla
onion	rose	varnish
orange	rosemary	vegetable
orange flower	rubber	verbena
oriental	rum	vermouth
orris	saffron	violet
oyster	sage	vinegar
ozone	sandalwood	walnut
paprika	sea-like	warm
parsley	seedy	watercress
patchouli	smoke	watermelon
peach	smooth	waxy
peanut	soapy	weedy
pencil	sour	wet dog
pepper	spearmint	wheat
peppermint	spicy	wintergreen
phlox	spirits	winy
pickles	straw	witch hazel
pine	strawberry	woodruff
pineapple	stringbean	woody
pistachio	sweat	yeast-like

Appendix VII
Olfactory Perception Test

This simple test will help you determine whether your sense of smell is better or worse than average. You might want to take the test at different times of day, and at different times of the month. Do it often and check for improvement in your ability to detect scents.

To do this test, you will need a friend, pure white vinegar, distilled water, four matching narrow-mouthed bottles (four- to eight-ounce size with lids), a china marker, an eyedropper, and measuring spoons.

The procedure is easy. You stay out of the room while your friend fills three of the bottles with distilled water and the fourth, which has been secretly marked with the china marker, with the vinegar. The lids are replaced and all spills are wiped up. You then remove the caps, sniff the liquids once and try to identify the one containing vinegar. Repeat this test, with your friend cutting the amount of vinegar in half each time and refilling the bottle with water.

Recognizing the vinegar through nine to twelve dilution steps is average. If your sense of smell is poor, or has been damaged, you may only proceed through three or four steps.

Appendix VIII
Standard Dilution Procedure

The perfumer's standard dilution procedure will help you learn the changes that take place when the strength of the scent is varied. It is useful when you begin to create perfumes and colognes, and as another type of olfactory test.

You will need four eyedroppers, four test tubes, a test-tube stand, and a fifth of 190-proof alcohol for each oil you are going to dilute. Usually you will not need to take the procedure to the dilution level of the fourth test tube, but you should understand how to complete the process.

Label the eyedroppers and test tubes in pairs: 1, 2, 3, and 4. Each dropper must handle solution from its matching test tube only. Set them in the stand.

Use dropper #1 to place ten drops of alcohol in test tube #1. Mark the liquid level with an indelible marker. Pour the liquid into test tube #2. Refill and repour from tube #1 (using the marked level) into tube #2 nine more times. Mark this level in test tube #2. You will have ten times the amount in tube #2 than in #1, or 100 drops. Pour the liquid from tube #2 into test tube #3. Proceed as before until you have poured a total of ten test tube #2 levels into tube #3. Test tube #3 will contain 1,000 drops. Mark the level. Follow the same procedure into test tube #4 which will then contain 10,000 drops. Go back and fill test tubes #1, #2, and #3 to their marked levels. Tube #1 will have 10 drops, tube #2 one hundred drops, tube #3 one thousand drops, and tube #4 ten thousand drops.

Now use eyedropper #1 to place one drop of essential oil into tube #1. This makes a one to ten solution. Again using dropper #1, take one drop of solution from test tube #1 and place it in tube #2. This creates a one to one thousand solution. Using dropper #2, place one drop solution from tube #2 into tube #3. This will make a one to one million solution. Finally, use dropper #3 to transfer one drop of solution from tube #3 to tube #4. This makes a one to one billion solution. Unless you are working with real musk or civet, the contents of tube #4 probably will not have a detectable odor.

Alternatively, stronger dilutions may be created. A one to one hundred solution is obtained by placing one drop of oil directly into test tube #2. One to one thousand and one to ten thousand dilutions are obtained by placing one drop of oil directly into tubes #3 and #4 respectively. Check the dilutions by putting one drop from each tube onto filter paper.

Appendix IX
Alcohol Dilution Chart

Occasionally you will come across a cologne or toilet water formula that requires a weaker strength alcohol than you have available. Dilute the alcohol with pure distilled water according to the following chart:

To Each Cup of 70% - 140 Proof Alcohol

Add water:	To make:
3 tablespoons	65% - 130 proof
4 tablespoons	60% - 120 proof
5 tablespoons	55% - 110 proof
6 tablespoons	50% - 100 proof

To Each Cup of 95% - 190 Proof Alcohol

Add water:	To make:
1 tablespoon	90% - 180 proof
2 tablespoons	85% - 170 proof
3 tablespoons	80% - 160 proof
5 tablespoons	75% - 150 proof
7 tablespoons	70% - 140 proof
½ cup	65% - 130 proof
½ cup + 1 tablespoon	60% - 120 proof
½ cup + 3 tablespoons	55% - 110 proof
¾ cup	50% - 100 proof

Appendix X
Sources of Essential Oils Used in Perfume

Essential oils are distilled, expressed, or gathered by the enfleurage method from many different sources.

Part or Type of Plant Used	To Obtain These Oils
balsam	capaiba, gilead, labdanum, Peru, and tolu
bark	birch, cascarilla, cassia, and cinnamon
buds and berries (dried)	allspice, clove, cubeb, and juniper
flowers	cananga, carnation, cassia, hyacinth, jasmine, mimosa, narcissus, neroli, reseda, rose, tuberose, violet, and ylang ylang
fruits (dried)	anise, coriander, fennel, juniper, and nutmeg
fruits (fresh)	almond, bergamot, citron, grapefruit, lemon, lime, mandarin, orange, and tangerine
grasses	citronella, ginger grass, lemongrass, and palmarosa
gums	elemi, frankincense, galbanum, mastic, myrrh, opoponax, and storax

Part or Type of Plant Used	To Obtain These Oils
herb (flowering plants)	basil, chamomile, clary sage, dill, fennel, geranium, lavender, lovage, marjoram, oregano, parsley, pennyroyal, peppermint, rosemary, rue, sage, spearmint, spike lavender, tansy, tarragon, thyme, verbena, wormseed, and wormwood
leaves	bay, cinnamon, eucalyptus, patchouli, petitgrain, thuja cedar, and wintergreen
leaves (dried)	cherry laurel, eucalyptus, niaouli, and patchouli
leaves, needles, and twigs	cajeput, cassia, cypress, and the pines—abies, siberica, silver, sylvestris, cedar
roots and rhizomes	angelica, calamus, costus, ginger, orris, valerian, and vetiver
seeds	ambrette, angelica, cardamom, carrot, croton, cumin, dill, mustard, and parsley
woods	amyris, birch, bois de rose, cade, camphor, cedar, guaiac, laurel, linaloe, sandalwood, santal, and sassafras

Appendix XI
The Secret Romantic Language of Flowers and Herbs

Long ago, bouquets were used to convey messages. The love-sick shepherd gathered flowers and herbs and left them for his favorite milkmaid, who was able to read his message from the types of plants he had given her. In China and Japan, bouquets served to send subtle political messages as well as a lover's message.

With the advent of literacy, the use of flowers as a way to communicate began to fade away. Today we use other forms of communication, but in times past, reading and writing belonged only to scholars. Common men and women communicated from a distance with plants from gardens, fields, meadows, and woods. Most of the plants had familiar meanings which were derived from use, culture, shape, folklore, or mythology. It often required some imagination to interpret the thought, but people of similar background had no difficulty conveying a simple message.

Although traditionally our culture has not attached underlying meanings to many of the materials used in potpourris, a list which follows has been compiled giving the interpretations of various flowers, leaves, seeds, roots, and oils. The traditional meanings are printed in italics and the meanings attributed by the

Garden Sage
Salvia officinalis

author appear in regular type.

When you intend to make a gift that will also serve as a message, refer to the list to discover which materials have the meanings you wish to communicate. Next, decide which of these have the best possibilities for developing into a fragrance product. Select other materials for their fragrance, even if their message is not the one you want to convey. Include a card with the gift explaining the meanings of the plant materials.

An example that might help you think in the "symbolic mode" would be a potpourri made mostly of red roses, orris, and woodruff, which could be interpreted as, "I love your enchanting spirit and cannot live without you." Peonies, calamus, coriander, and other materials would mean, "I am too shy to express my inner feelings."

Use your imagination to add messages to your spring bouquets and winter potpourri and double the pleasure your gifts will bring.

	Meaning	Fragrance	Color
acacia	*friendship*	fragrant	yellow
alfalfa leaf	ponder, ruminate, consider	hay scent	yellow-green
African violet	*such worth is rare*	variable	white, pink, yellow, purple
allspice berries and oil	valuable, precious	spicy, clovy	dark brown
almond (flowering)	*hope*	sweet	white
almond oil (bitter)	dangerous, risky	sweet and bitter	
amaryllis	*pride, splendid beauty, timidity*	fragrant	white, reds, oranges
ambergris	enjoyable arousal	delicate, earthy	yellowish
ambrette seed	desirous	musky	small black seeds
anemone	*forsaken*	delicate	reds, white, purples

	Meaning	Fragrance	Color
angelica root	celestial	woody, celery seed	white-brown
anise seed and oil	indulgence, repletion	sweet candy	yellow-tan
apple blossom and oil	*preference*	sweet	white
apricot scent	concupiscence	sweet, heady	
arbor vitae	*unchanging friendship, live for me*	aromatic	deep green
arnica flowers	unsure, unclear	delicate	tan-brown, fuzzy texture
aster, Chinese	*variety, afterthought*	variable	all colors
auricula	*painting*	fragrant	yellow
azalea	*temperance*	fragrant	pinks, red-violets
bachelor's button	*celibacy*	slight	blue
balm of Gilead buds	*sympathy, consolation*	sweet, balsamic	red-brown

	Meaning	Fragrance	Color
balsam of Peru oil	melancholy	light, resinous	
balsam of Tolu oil	revery	airy, resinous	
basil leaf and oil	*love, hate, a guide to paradise*	warm, aromatic	light to dark green
bay leaf and oil	*victory, glory, I change but in death*	sweet pungency	yellow-green
bayberry bark	industry	bitter, spicy	medium brown
begonia	*deformity*	sweet	white, red, yellow, purple
belladonna	*silence, hush*	rank	violet or greenish
bellflower	*gratitude*	fragrant	white or blue
benzoin gum	preserve, dole out	sweet, aromatic	white to dark brown
bergamot oil	sprightly, dexterous	pungent citrus	
birch oil	piercing love	wintergreen	

	Meaning	Fragrance	Color
blackberry leaf	wounded	faint, sweet	dark green
blueberry leaf	obscure, wild	neutral	light green
borage leaf and flowers	*courage, cheerful, merry*	faint cucumber	green
broom flowers	*humility*	sweet	yellow-orange, orange-brown
burnet leaf	*lighthearted*	cucumber	green
cactus flowers	*warmth*	sweet	white-yellow
cajeput oil	revivify	evergreen, camphor	
calamus root	communication, luxury	spicy, woody	tan-brown
calceolaria	*I offer you my fortune*	slight	red to yellow
calcatrippae flowers	shyness	faint hay-honey	purple
calendula blossoms	*grief, cruelty in love*	aromatic	yellow-orange

	Meaning	Fragrance	Color
camelia	*unpretending excellence*	sweet	red
camelia	*reflected loveliness*	sweet	white
Canada snakeroot	*timidity*	gingery	tan
canary grass	*perseverance*	grassy	dark green
candytuft	*indifference*	fragrant	white, purple
caraway seed and oil	*cure for fickleness, steadfast*	aromatic	green-brown
cardamon seed	*treasure*	spicy, pungent	green-white
carnation flower oil	*adventurous love*	sweet, spicy	
castoreum	*uncontrollable love*	leathery	
catnip	*courage, intoxicating love*	hay-mint	green
cedarwood and oil	*protection, preservation*	woody, aromatic	red-brown

	Meaning	Fragrance	Color
celery seed	gustatory delight	spicy	green-brown
chamomile	patience, *humility*	faint pineapple	white or yellow
chestnut tree	*do me justice*	slight	yellow
chicory	*frugality*	slight	blue
chrysanthemum	*I love*	some	red
chrysanthemum	*absolute truth, fidelity*	some	white
chrysanthemum	*slighted love*	some, spicy	yellow, orange
cineraria	*always delightful*	fragrant	all colors
cinnamon chips and oil	esteem, favor	spicy, sweet	orange-brown
citronella oil	keep away, don't be a pest	pungent citrus	
civet oil	seductive	sweet, delicate	
clary sage oil	supportive	pleasant	

	Meaning	Fragrance	Color
clematis	*beauty of mind*	fragrant	white, blues, purples
clove buds and oil	cherish	spicy, aromatic	red-brown
clover (four leaf)	*be mine*, luck	fresh, grassy	green
clover (red)	industry	sweet hay	pink-brown
clover	*think of me*	sweet hay	white-tan
coconut scent	generosity	very fragrant	
coltsfoot	*maternal care*	none	green-brown
coreopsis flowers	*cheerful*	faint	all colors
coriander seed and oil	*hidden merit*	spicy, aromatic	tan
costus root	express your sensuality	musky	tan-brown
cowslips	*divine beauty*	fragrant	all colors
crocus	*abuse not, merriment*	fresh	yellow, white, purple

	Meaning	Fragrance	Color
cubeb berries	piquant	peppery	black
cumin	*faithfulness, fidelity, marriage*	bitter, pungent	green-brown
cypress	*death, mourning*	aromatic	dark green
daffodil	*high regard*	sweet	white, yellow
dahlia	*instability*	faint	white
daisy	*innocence*	some	white
daisy	*beauty*	faint	all colors
dandelion	*oracle*	faint	yellow
daphne odora	*painting the lily*	fragrant	pink
deer tongue leaves	*have a heart*	sweet, vanilla	dark green
dew plant	*a serenade*	some	white, pink
dill seed and oil	*magical charm, luck*	aromatic	brown-green

	Meaning	Fragrance	Color
eglantine foliage	*simplicity*	apple-scented	green
eglantine flowers	*poetry, I wound to heal*	fragrant	pink
elder berries and flowers	*compassion, death, magic*	honey	purple berries, yellow bloom
eucalyptus leaf and oil	*get well, take care of yourself*	pungent, aromatic	light yellow-green
everlasting	*never-ceasing remembrance*	curry	yellow
fennel seed and oil	*flattery*	licorice, spicy	yellow-green
fenugreek seed	*honey sweet, mellifluous*	sweet, pungent	orange-brown
fern	*fascination, magic, sincerity*	woodsy	green
fir oil, Siberian	*time, revitalize, inspire*	pungent, evergreen	
flax	*appreciation*	faint	blue

	Meaning	Fragrance	Color
forget-me-not	true love, pure love, faithfulness	some	yellow-blue
foxglove	sincerity	negligible	all colors
frankincense	worship	incense	yellow-white
fumitory plant	hatred	strong	green-brown
fuschia	impeccable taste, fast	some	red-violets, corals
galangal root	gallant	pungent, tart	red-brown (burnt sienna)
gardenia flowers and oil	secret untold love	heady, sweet	white
geranium (ivy)	bridal favor	slight	green
geranium (lemon)	unexpected meeting	lemon	lavender
geranium (nutmeg)	expected meeting	spicy	green foliage
geranium (red)	friendship, be comforted	geranium	red
geranium (silver leaf)	recall	faint	green foliage

	Meaning	Fragrance	Color
gillyflower	bond of affection	sweet	yellow
ginger root and oil	tender, delectable	spicy, strong	yellow-brown
gladiolus	strong character	some	all colors
globe amaranth	immortality, unfading love	neutral scent	red-violet
grapefruit oil	waning, wasting	pungent citrus	
hawthorne flowers and berries	hope, betrothal, marriage	pleasant	deep red berries, white flowers
heather	admiration, protection	slight, sweet	purple
heliotrope flowers and oil	admiration, protection, eternal love	sweet, cherry	white or purple flowers
henna	alteration, improvement	fragrant	greenish
hibiscus	delicate beauty, flirtatious	faint, sweet	dark red

	Meaning	Fragrance	Color
honeysuckle	generous and devoted affection	sweet	yellow
honeysuckle	the color of my fate	sweet	coral
hop flowers	sweet dreams	pungent hay	delicate green
horehound	health	some	dark green
hova	sculpture	fragrant	pink
hyacinth	sports, games, play	very fragrant	blue
hyacinth	sorrowful	very fragrant	purple
hyacinth	unobtrusive loveliness	very fragrant	white
hydrangea	a boaster	some	all colors
hyssop	sacrifice	faint hay-herbal	
ice plants	your looks freeze me	none	all colors
iris	a messenger	faint	blue

	Meaning	Fragrance	Color
iris	*flame, I burn*	sweet	red
ivy	*faithful friendship, fidelity, marriage*	fresh	dark green
jasmine flowers and oil	*amiability, sensuality, grace, and elegance*	very sweet	white
juniper berries and oil	*delectable*	aromatic	purple-black
kesu flowers	*gleeful*	slightly aromatic	yellow-orange
king-cups	*desire for riches*	slight	yellow
labdanum oil	*hidden value*	sweet resin	
lantana	*rigor*	slight	yellow
larkspur	*lightness, levity, fickleness*	some	blue
laurestina	*a token*	fresh	white

	Meaning	Fragrance	Color
lavender	*silence, distrust, protect*	aromatic	purple
leaves (dry)	*melancholy*	none	red, yellow, brown
lemon balm	*memories, longevity, sympathy*	lemony	dark green
lemon blossoms	*fidelity in love*	sweet	pale yellow
lemongrass and oil	*envy, jealousy*	lemony-aspirin	light yellow-green
lemon peel	*zest, tart*	intense citrus	yellowish
lemon thyme	*belated*	herbal citrus	bright green
lemon verbena	*delicacy of feeling*	lemon aromatic	medium green
licorice mint	*eschew*	anise-like	tan-dark green
licorice root	*sweet and soothing*	sweet, rooty	brown
lilac	*first emotions of love, awakening love*	fragrant	purple

	Meaning	Fragrance	Color
lilac	*youthful innocence*	fragrant	white
lily (imperial)	*majesty*	fresh	white
lily (madonna)	*purity, sweetness*	fresh	white
lily	*crime*	fresh	yellow
lily-of-the-valley flowers and oil	*return of happiness*	fragrant	white
linden leaves and flowers	*scintillating*	faintly sweet	light green
lobelia	*malevolence*	rank	reds, blues
lotus flowers and oil	*eloquence, mystery, truth, eternity*	heady sweet	white
lovage root	*hidden virtues*	light	brownish
lupine	*voraciousness*	fresh	all colors
mace	*embrace, cling to me*	spicy	red-brown

118

	Meaning	Fragrance	Color
magnolia flowers and oil	*love of nature*	sweet	white
malva	*renunciaton, sorrow*	slight	black
malva	*ambition, fertility*	slight	blue-purple
marjoram leaf and oil	*happiness, health*	herbal, aromatic	grey-green
marshmallow root	*beneficence*	woody	tan
mignonette	*your qualities surpass your charms*	very fragrant	yellow, red
mock orange	*counterfeit*	fragrant	white
motherwort	*fertility*	aromatic	dark green
mugwort	*forgetfulness, weary traveler*	pungent	green-brown
musk oil	*erotic effects*	very fragrant	
myrrh gum	*adoration*	sweet, aromatic	brownish

	Meaning	Fragrance	Color
myrtle	*love*	fragrant	white, pink
narcissus	*egotism, self-centered*	fragrant	white, yellow
nasturtium	*patriotic*	spicy, peppery	yellow, orange
nettle	*you are spiteful, slander, cruelty*	none	green
nutmeg	*your love is a drug*	spicy	brown
oak moss	*ardent love*	sweet	silvery-grey
oleander	*beware*	vanilla	rose
olive	*peace*	tonic odor	green
orange blossom	*your purity equals your loveliness*	sweet	orange
orange flowers	*chastity, bridal festivities*	sweet	white

	Meaning	Fragrance	Color
orange peel	virve	orange, dry	orangish
orchid	*beauty, magnificence*	fresh	all colors
oregano	bitter	pungent	grey-green
orris root	enchanting spirit, angelic	sweet, violet	white-tan
pansy	*thoughts*	sweet	all colors
parsley	*festivity, victory, death, the beginning*	pungent	green
passion flower	*faith*	fresh	yellow
patchouli leaf and oil	decadence	earthy, pungent	dark green-black
peach blossom	*I am your captive*	fragrant	bright pink
pennyroyal leaf and oil	*flee away*	soft mint	green
peony flower and root	*shy, bashful*	fragrant	pink, red, white
peppermint leaf and oil	*wisdom, strength*	aromatic mint	dark green

	Meaning	Fragrance	Color
periwinkle	*early friendship*	some	blue
petunia	*your presence soothes me*	sweet at night	all colors
pine cones	*outdoors*	none	brown
pine needle oil	*exhilarating*	pungent aromatic	
pink	*boldness*	fragrant	all colors
pink, carnation	*woman's love*	fragrant	all colors
pink, clove	*resignation*	spicy	pink
pink, Indian double	*always lovely*	fragrant	red
pink, Indian single	*aversion*	fragrant	red
pink, double	*pure and ardent love*	fragrant	red
pink, single	*talent, ingenuity*	fragrant	all colors
plumbago, larpenta	*holy wishes*	faint	blue

	Meaning	Fragrance	Color
poppy	oblivion, consolation	faint	red
poppy	sleep	faint	white
primrose	early youth and sadness	balmy	all colors
raspberry leaf	motherhood	lightly sweet	grey-green
reindeer moss	icy	sweet, dry	
rhododendron	danger, beware	fragrant	all colors
rose	love, passionate love	fragrant	red
rose	bashful shame	fragrant	deep red
rose	I am worthy of you, silence	fragrant	white
rose	unity	fragrant	red and white
rose	infidelity, decreased love, jealousy	fragrant	yellow

	Meaning	Fragrance	Color
rose (bridal)	*happy love*	fragrant	white
rose (cabbage)	*ambassador of love, true love*	fragrant	pink or white
rose (centifolia)	*grace*	fragrant	red or pink
rose (daily)	*I aspire to thy smile*	fragrant	any color
rose (damask)	*brilliant complexion*	fragrant	white or striped
rose (musk)	*capricious love*	musky	red
rose (single)	*simplicity*	slight	pink
rose (thornless)	*early attachment*	slight	any color
rose (withered)	*transient impressions*	slight	white
rosebud	*pure and lovely*	fragrant	red
rosebud	*girlhood*	fragrant	white
rosebud	*confession of love*	slight	moss

	Meaning	Fragrance	Color
rosehips	fruit of love	slight	red
rose geranium oil	illusion	rosy	
rosemary leaf and oil	*friendship, fidelity, invigorating*	pungent, aromatic	grey-green
rue leaf	*remorse, repentance, grace*	aromatic	green
safflower	imitation	aromatic	red-orange
sage leaf and oil	*immortality, esteem, wit, wisdom*	aromatic, pungent	grey-green
Saint John's wort	*animosity*		
salvia	wisdom	spicy	blue
salvia	energy	spicy	red
sandalwood chips and oil	reincarnation, continuance	woody, aromatic	yellow-tan
sarsaparilla root	tonic	woody, rooty	yellow-tan

	Meaning	Fragrance	Color
sassafras root bark and oil	sassy, you are a tease	spicy, root beer	red-brown
saw palmetto berries	lost	acidic	dark brown
senna leaf	renunciation, avoidance	stable	yellow-green
sensitive plant	*sensibility*	fragrant	yellow, purple
snowdrops	*hopefulness*	slight	white
sorrel	*parental affection*	acid, lemony	green
southernwood	constancy, *lad's love*	aromatic	green-brown
spearmint leaf and oil	relaxation, refreshment	aromatic mint	green
speedwell	*fidelity*	violet	pale violet
spikenard root	precious, abnegation	fragrant	tan-brown
spina cristi	ephemeral	hay, sweet	pale orange

	Meaning	Fragrance	Color
spruce oil	festivity	aromatic, evergreen	
star anise	fate	spicy, pungent	brown
stock	*lasting beauty*	sweet	all colors
stonecrop	*tranquility*		
storax oil	depression	low, aromatic	
strawberry leaf	*righteous*	neutral hay-herbal	green
strawberry oil	*righteous*	sweet, fruity	
sumac berries	slake	acid, tart	red
sunflower	*constancy in love, false riches, haughty*	slight	yellow
sweet pea	*delicate pleasures*	sweet	all colors
syringa	*memory*	none	violet

	Meaning	Fragrance	Color
tangerine oil	vivacious	sweet citrus	
tansy leaf	*hostile thoughts, repellent*	aromatic	green-brown
tarragon leaf and oil	appealing	spicy	green
thistle	*austerity*	none	green
thorn branch	*severity*	none	brown
thrift	*sympathy*	slight	pink
thuja cedar leaf oil	intense	aromatic, evergreen	
thyme	*activity, bravery, time, infinity*	pungent herbal	dark green-brown
tilia star flowers	unyielding	slight	orange-brown
tonka beans	beauteous	sweet, vanilla	black
tuberose	*dangerous pleasures*	fragrant	white

128

	Meaning	Fragrance	Color
tulip	*declaration of love*	none	red
tulip	*beautiful eyes*	none	variegated
tulip	*hopeless love*	none	yellow
uva ursi	*amplify*	slight	green
valerian flowers and root	*readiness, antagonism*	rank	purple
vanilla bean	*ethereal*	sweet	dark brown
verbena	*family union*	fragrant	pink
verbena	*united against evil*	fragrant	scarlet
verbena	*pray for me*	fragrant	white
vervain	*enchantment*	aromatic	pink-blue
vetiver root and oil	*shield, screen*	woody, aromatic	orange-brown
violet flower	*faithfulness, loyalty*	faint, sweet	blue

	Meaning	Fragrance	Color
violet flower	*innocence, modesty*	sweet	white
violet leaf and oil	charming	sweet, violet	green
wallflower	*fidelity in adversity*	sweet	all colors
white thyme oil	for all time	aromatic	
wild cherry bark	truthfulness	faint	reds
willow (weeping)	*mourning*	fresh	green
wintergreen leaf and oil	refreshing	aromatic	green-brown
wisteria	*welcome, fair stranger*	sweet	violet blue
wood betony plant	*holy, sanctify, surprise*	sweet, delicate	dark and light green
woodruff	life in death	vanilla-hay	green-brown
wormwood	*absence, displeasure*	aromatic	green-tan
xanthium (cocklebur)	*rudeness, pertinacity*	none	green

	Meaning	Fragrance	Color
yarrow flowers	*incantations, foretelling the future*	slight	white–yellow
yerba santa leaf	*saintly*	slight, sweet	gray-green
yew	*sorrow*	woody, evergreen	green
zinnia	*thoughts of absent friends*	fresh	all colors

NOTES

NOTES

NOTES

NOTES